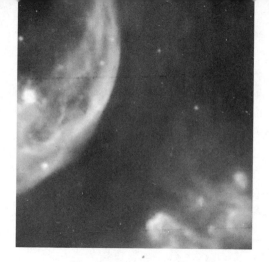

EDGAR CAYCE

AND THE

COSMOS

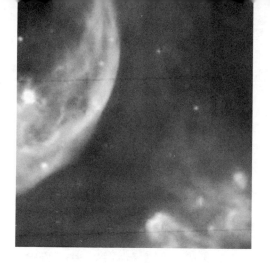

EDGAR CAYCE
AND THE
COSMOS

James Mullaney

**ASSOCIATION FOR
RESEARCH AND
ENLIGHTENMENT**

A.R.E. Press • Virginia Beach • Virginia

A.R.E. Press
215 67th Street
Virginia Beach, VA 23451-2061

Library of Congress Cataloging-in-Publication Data
Mullaney, James.
  Edgar Cayce and the cosmos / by James Mullaney.
      p.   cm.
  Includes index.
  ISBN 13: 978-0-87604-566-4 (trade pbk.)
    1. Parapsychology and science. 2. Cayce, Edgar, 1877-1945. 3. Cosmol-
ogy. I. Title.
  BF1045.S33M85 2007
  133.8092—dc22
                                        2007019709
                  Cover design by Richard Boyle

Images reproduced in the center spread are courtesy of NASA, the Space Telescope Science Institute and the Hubble Heritage Team, and the European Space Agency (ESA).

DEDICATION

To my dear wife, Sharon McDonald Mullaney, for her patience and encouragement during the long process of researching and writing this book. Edgar Cayce's work has double meaning for both of us, since it was at an A.R.E. conference that fate brought us together.

CONTENTS

Centerspread Photo Gallery:
Hubble Space Telescope Sites and Images

ACKNOWLEDGMENTS

Many people helped to make this book possible. It was the A.R.E.'s John Van Auken who first suggested using my astronomical background to explore what Edgar Cayce had to say in his readings about the amazing cosmos in which we live. A.R.E. Press Senior Editor, Ken Skidmore, has been a sincere pleasure to work with throughout this project. I'm also grateful to A. Robert Smith, former editor of *Venture Inward*, for publishing my articles over the years within its pages—in particular, that entitled "Divine Order in the Universe" which appeared in the September/October 2002 issue. The enthusiastic response it elicited from readers worldwide was partly responsible for the eventual appearance of this book. My thanks also go to Leslie Cayce for inviting me to share the wonders of the cosmos at many A.R.E. conferences (both through slide-illustrated lectures and stargazing sessions with my telescope). I am particularly indebted to the Space Telescope Science Institute in Baltimore for use of the stunning Hubble Space Telescope images which grace the centerspread section of this book—and to Charles Feldman, a retired engineer, for kindly downloading them onto CD-ROMs for me. I also wish to acknowledge my dear friends and longtime A.R.E. members, Marge and Warren Greenwald. Attending their Search for God Study Group meetings (West Chester, Pennsylvania, #1—which they conducted for nearly thirty years!), as well as through many private discussions, provided valuable insights into the Cayce material in general. And while this book is already dedicated to my wonderful wife, Sharon, I must acknowledge again here the invaluable role she played in my completion of this project.

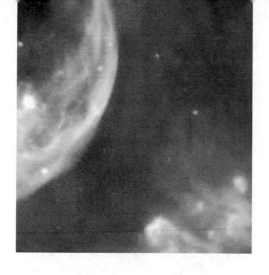

Preface

> "God is reflected in our concept of space. In the vastness of space our self-conceit falters. We are humblest when gazing at the stars. We draw nearer to God in contemplation of the immensity of the universe."   (*A Search for God*, Book II)

When I first heard about Edgar Cayce over forty years ago, I approached his psychic readings with skepticism, coming as I did from the standpoint of one trained in the physical sciences (mainly astronomy and physics). Even earlier than my encounter with the Cayce material was that with the momentous issues of UFOs and extraterrestrial life. As both an amateur and professional astronomer, I had no doubt about the existence of life elsewhere in this vast universe. But here, too, I harbored a degree of skepticism—particularly in the case of some of the UFO sightings. While scientific training demands critical thinking and rigorous proof of any new theories put forth or reports of unusual phenomena, I came to realize that such a formal background can also in many situations blind a person to the deeper realities lying behind nature. With further study of both the Cayce material and the UFO phenomenon, I soon lost all skepticism about either of them!

In the pages to follow, we'll look briefly at the man Edgar Cayce and at the amazing Cayce psychic readings, which contain a truly vast storehouse of information about many subjects, including the universe itself.

Edgar Cayce, often called the Sleeping Prophet of Virginia Beach, was without question one of the greatest psychics the world has ever known. This simple soul was a devoted family man, a photographer, and an avid gardener. Deeply spiritual, he read the Bible daily and was a Sunday school teacher. From most appearances, he was just an ordinary person of his time.

Yet, for more than forty years of his adult life, he displayed the phenomenal ability to put himself into a trancelike sleep at will and give psychic discourses, called *readings*. By stretching out on a couch, folding his hands over his stomach, and closing his eyes, he would enter a relaxed state from which he was able to place his mind in contact with the "Akashic records" of the cosmos.[1] He would then answer questions, put to him by his wife or another close associate, from people all over the world, concerning their past lives, mission on planet Earth, medical conditions, and a host of other subjects about which Cayce in his conscious state could not possibly have known. Amazingly, when he did awaken from his trances, he remembered *nothing* about what he had said or what had transpired!

Edgar Cayce was born on a farm outside of Hopkinsville, Kentucky, on March 18, 1877. He died in Virginia Beach, Virginia, on January 3, 1945, at the age of 67, leaving behind thousands of psychic readings, copies of which are preserved at the headquarters of the Association for Research and Enlightenment (A.R.E.), an organization that he founded in 1931.

Cayce Biographies

Even though it's now been over six decades since Edgar Cayce passed on, the timeless value of his readings has brought ever-increasing numbers of seekers to the A.R.E. over the years to study the priceless treasure trove he gave the world. Countless articles and papers and hundreds of books have been written about him! Several television specials about his life and work have also aired nationally. Among the most popular of the biographies that have been published about Edgar Cayce are the following four titles:

- *There Is a River*, Thomas Sugrue (1942)
- *Many Mansions*, Gina Cerminara (1950)
- *The Sleeping Prophet*, Jess Stearn (1967)
- *Edgar Cayce: An American Prophet*, Sidney Kirkpatrick (2000)

The Amazing Cayce Readings

Upon Edgar Cayce's death, Gladys Davis, Cayce's long-time secretary, dedicated herself to preserving and organizing the readings, undertaking the enormous task of cataloging and indexing a total of more than 14,000 of them. She found that nearly every imaginable question on some 10,000 different subjects had been put to Cayce! Due to the sheer number of readings, plus follow-up reports and documentation, she did not complete the indexing project until 1971. Copies of the original readings are still preserved in the A.R.E. library for study, and they also have been available for some time now on a CD-ROM. They represent the largest collection of psychic information from a single source in the world today.

For more than a century, the Cayce readings have been explored by individuals from every possible background. They have been intently studied by professionals in the fields of medicine, nutrition, science, education, theology, psychology, and even history. Cayce's pioneering emphasis on the importance of diet, mental attitude, emotions, exercise, and even prayer and spirituality in the treatment of illness earned him recognition by medical practitioners as "the father of holistic medicine." Psychologists have compared him to Carl Jung and educators to Rudlolf Steiner. A famed religious scholar, author, and retired academician, Richard Drummond, Ph.D., referred to the Cayce readings as "the finest devotional material of the twentieth century." Historical insights that the readings provided into early Christianity and Judaism were subsequently verified only long after Cayce's time. And as will be seen in this book, the information contained in the readings on sciences like astronomy, cosmology, and physics is simply astounding! (This information is examined further in the section "An Astounding Revelation" in Appendix 3.)

Many have described the language used by Edgar Cayce in his readings as strange, odd, cryptic, rambling, redundant, and/or difficult to understand. This is perhaps not unexpected, given the source of the readings (as explained later). A wonderful article on the nature of this language by Dr. Gina Cerminara, one of his biographers, originally appeared in the *A.R.E. Bulletin* for December, 1945, and was later reprinted in the April 1966 issue of *The A.R.E. Journal*. It is given in full in Appendix 2.

And now, dear reader, together let's embark upon our exciting cosmic journey—not only through the eyes of the Hubble Space Telescope and the latest discoveries in the physical sciences, but also through those of the most amazing psychic the world has ever known!

James Mullaney
Rehoboth Beach, Delaware
U.S.A, Planet Earth

---

[1]Perhaps the ultimate reference about these records is Kevin Todeschi's superb *Edgar Cayce on the Akashic Records*, available from the A.R.E. Press.

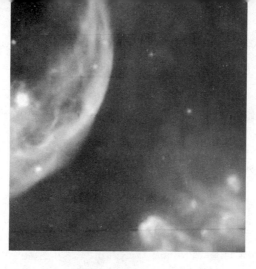

1

Worlds Beyond:
Stars and Stellar Systems

THE COSMIC HIERARCHY

Before looking at some of the many references to stars and stellar systems contained within the Cayce readings, let's say a few words about the cosmic scheme of things. We are living in a vast pinwheel of stars known as the Milky Way Galaxy, which is only one of an estimated *100 billion galaxies* within the observable universe! Although Edgar Cayce didn't specifically mention the Milky Way[2] or other galaxies in his readings, he did talk about "other universes." Some of these may very well be references to other galaxies.[3]

Stars themselves are born within immense clouds of hydrogen gas in the spiral arms of galaxies, becoming ever hotter and more compressed as they condense out of these rotating nebulous masses. (As related later, Cayce actually mentions these "nebulae" and talks about the "mists that are gathering" as part of the creation process.) Like spinning ice skaters pulling their arms in close to their body, the protostars spin faster and faster as they become ever smaller, and if something doesn't slow them down, they'll eventually tear themselves apart. Even as the skaters slow their spin by throwing out their arms, these infant stars in essence do the same thing by shedding rings of material, which act like stellar brakes. This material in turn forms the planets and their satellites. It's been statistically calculated that there are more stars within reach of today's largest telescopes than all the grains of sand on all the beaches and deserts on the entire planet Earth. And we now know that virtually all of those stars must have planets as a result of their natural birth process, so we're talking about a lot of worlds out there!

Most if not all stars are born in families. These range from orbiting double and multiple systems in which two or more suns (often of different lovely colors!) would appear in the skies of their planets, to clusters of stars—glittering stellar jewelboxes containing hundreds or thousands of suns to as many as a million in huge stellar beehivelike swarms. Our Sun is a star—our "Daytime Star" as many like to call it. And while it appears to be single, it's believed that it may actually have a very dim distant red–dwarf companion, slowly drifting through space with it. (At the opposite extreme are double stars orbiting so close to each that they complete a mutual revolution in a matter of just *hours* and their outer atmospheres are actually in contact!)

Stars Named in the Readings

While references to the stars appear hundreds of times in the Cayce material, only two appear to actually be mentioned by name. One of these is Polaris, better known as the North Star or Pole Star. Within the text of the readings it appears only three times, in the following contexts:

> For, as long as an entity is within the confines of that termed the earth's and the sons [suns?] of the earth's solar system, the developments are within the sojourns of the entity from sphere to sphere; and when completed it begins—throughout the music of the spheres with Arcturus, Polaris, and through those sojourns in the outer sphere.   441-1

(This reading actually does mention the other named star—Arcturus—and also the "music of the spheres," both of which are discussed below.)

At the correct time accurate imaginary lines can be drawn from the opening of the great Pyramid to the second star in the Great Dipper, called Polaris or the North Star. This indicates it is the system toward which the soul takes it flight after having completed its sojourn through this solar system. 5748-6

(Note that Cayce referred to Polaris as the second star in the "Great Dipper," which means the Big Dipper. But it's actually located at the end of the handle of the Little Dipper. This has always caused the author to puzzle over this particular reading. It *is* off the top—or second—star at the end of the bowl of the Big Dipper, which may well be what Cayce meant.)

In the lead of these, with those changes that had been as the promptings from the positions of the stars—that stand as it were in the dividing of the ways between the universal, that is the common vision of the solar system of the sun, and those from without the spheres—or as the common name, the North Star, as its variation made for those cycles that would be incoordinant with those changes that had been determined by some—this began the preparation— for the three hundred years, as has been given, in this period.

In these signs then was the new cycle, that as was then— as we have in the astrological—the beginning of the Piscean age, or that position of the Polar Star or North Star as related to the southern clouds. These made for the signs, these made for the symbols; as would be the sign as used, the manner of the sign's approach and the like. 5749-8

There are two very important astronomical terms contained in this last reading worth noting. The variation in the position of Polaris that's mentioned is a direct reference to the Precession of the Equinoxes resulting from the slow wobbling of the Earth on its axis. The other one is "southern clouds." It was mentioned earlier that Cayce didn't speak of other galaxies as such. However, the term "southern clouds" is a reference to the two "Magellanic Clouds" visible only from the Southern Hemisphere. These are, in fact, our Milky Way's satellite galaxies!

The "Stargate" Arcturus

The other star that Edgar Cayce specifically mentioned by name is the radiant golden–orange sun Arcturus. Best seen in the spring sky, it's the third brightest of the heavenly host visible from the Northern Hemisphere after the blue–white gems Sirius and Vega (which are best seen in the winter and summer sky, respectively). This great star is referenced more than thirty times within the text of the readings alone, all having the theme of its supreme importance both individually and cosmically. Here's a sampling of those readings:

> Also we find the Sun and Arcturus, the greater Sun, giving
> of the strength in mental and spiritual elements toward
> developing of soul and of the attributes toward the better
> forces in earth's spheres.   137-4

> (Q) From the information received from this source, I am
> from Arcturian influences. What is this influence in my
> present experience?
> (A) As just indicated, and is as a part of that. For Arcturus
> is that junction between the spheres of activity as related to
> cosmic force, and is that about which this particular environ
> or sphere of activity rotates, or is a relative source of
> activity.   263-15

> As an entity passes on, as has been given, from this present—

or *this* solar system, *this* sun, *these* forces, it passes through the various spheres—leading first into that central force, through which—known as Arcturus—nearer the Pleiades, in this passage about the various spheres—on and *on*—through the *eons* of time, as called—or space—which is *one* in the various spheres of its activity . . .   311-2

(The Pleiades Star Cluster that's mentioned is discussed below.)

In those experiences of the entity in its dwellings in the hills and the plains of Persia, also in Egypt, the beauties and music of the spheres sang and brought into the experience of the entity its studies of the light by day, the joy of the voices of the night, and the star that led the entity— that source from which and to which it may gain so much of its strength in the present; Arcturus, the wonderful, the beautiful! As the bright and *glorious* light from same set afire, as it were, its meditations in the plains, so may the illuminations do the same in the lives of those the entity contacts through its gentleness and kindness and service.
827-1

Arcturus comes in this entity's chart, or as a central force from which the entity came again into the earth-material sojourns. For, this is the way, the door out of this system.
2454-3

Not that the sun that is the center of this solar system is all there is. For the entity has attained to that realm even of Arcturus, or that center from which there may be the entrance into other realms of consciousness.   2823-1

And Arcturus! For the entity has gone out and returned, purposefully.   5259-1

(Q) The sixth problem concerns interplanetary and inter-system dwelling, between earthly lives. It was given through this source that the entity Edgar Cayce, after the experience as Uhjltd, went to the system of Arcturus, and then returned to earth. Does this indicate a usual or an unusual step in soul evolution?
(A) As indicated, or as has been indicated in other sources besides this as respecting this very problem—Arcturus is that which may be called the center of this universe, through which individuals pass and at which period there comes the choice of the individual as to whether it is to return to complete there—that is, in this planetary system, our sun, the earth sun and its planetary system—or to pass on to others. This was an unusual step, and yet a usual one.
5749-14

And we find that the experience of the entity before that, as Uhjltd, was from even without the sphere of thine own orb; for the entity came from those centers about which thine own solar system moves—in Arcturus.   5755-1

As many of these readings make clear, Arcturus is definitely a "stargate" leading to other parts of the universe—even to its very center—and that it was actually used by Edgar Cayce himself! On a personal note, one of my wife's brothers was a brilliant young college student in the pre-med program at St. Joseph's University in Philadelphia. In 1970, tragically David was killed by a drunken driver. Until we met, Sharon had little interest in or knowledge about the stars, her passion being mathematics and music. Yet she somehow instinctively or psychically knew that her dear brother had gone to Arcturus! Incidentally, David himself was an avid stargazer and very much into space and astronomy. Just a coincidence? I think not!

Before going on, it should be pointed out that Sirius (mentioned above) is indirectly referred to by Edgar Cayce as "the dog star," which is its popular name due to its location in the constellation of Canis Major or the Big Dog. Other indirect references to stars in the readings are the "evening star" and especially the "morning star" (or "the bright and morning star" as he was fond of saying)—in both cases actually referring to the radiant planet Venus in its evening and morning appearances at dusk and dawn, respectively. Although Venus is a planet and not a star, these again are the popular names that have been given to it. And, while in fact the famed "Star of Bethlehem" (also called "His Star") is mentioned in the readings, this pertains to no actual named star in the sky today. Many astronomers believe that this was actually a supernova explosion—the death–throes of a supermassive sun that lit up the heavens for many weeks around the time of Christ's birth. (If this is indeed its true identity, the author finds it ironic that God would use the spectacular death of a star to announce the birth of the greatest King that ever lived.)

Personification of the Stars

There's a long tradition of poets, writers, visionaries, and even some scientists referring to the stars as if they are living entities rather than just inanimate matter as is widely believed. Indeed, as will be discussed in the next chapter, there are even those astronomers who believe that we're actually living in a "bio–cosmos" and that the universe itself is a colossal living "organism"! This idea has such profound implications if true that it's well worth examining it further before looking at what Edgar Cayce had to say about it. Here are several of the author's favorite literary references to what I personally believe to be an actual fact (based on communing with the stars for more than fifty years as a stargazer):

> "But every night come out these envoys of beauty, and light the universe with their admonishing smile."
> (Ralph Waldo Emerson)

> "I never behold the stars that I do not feel that I am looking into the face of God."   (Abraham Lincoln)

"The stars we love best are the ones into whose faces we can look for an hour at a time, if our fancy so leads us."
(Martha Evans Martin)

"A star looks down at me, and says: 'Here I and you stand, each in our own degree: What do you mean to do?'"
(Thomas Hardy)

"More beautiful, the stars in the vault of heaven remain watching over mankind asleep."   (Maria Valtorta)

"We have enjoyed knowing the stars. We are among the thousands who have found them old friends, to which we can turn time after time for refreshing thoughts and relief from the worries and troubles of every-day life."
(Dorothy Bennett, Hubert Bernhard, and Hugh Rice)

"The stars bind together all men and all periods of the world's history. As they have seen all from the beginning of time, so shall they see all that will come hereafter."
(Alexander von Humboldt)

Over the years, the author has been told by a number of people that Edgar Cayce claimed that when we pass on we become stars. While I haven't actually found a direct statement to that effect in the Cayce material, there are at least two indirect references to this in the readings (the italicized emphases being mine):

As to the astrological aspects for the entity, these are not influencing because the entity was born under this or that sign, this or that planet or star being in a certain or given position. It is true that there is a guide or guard for each and every entity or soul, or a developing influence that may be from *the entity's own activities as a new star in the universe.* [Author's emphasis]   1695-1

Ye can sow seeds and work them in self, but God gives the increase. He adds those that should be added from the activities of their own opportunities, *such as are worthy of becoming stars,* yea, even as blossoms in the garden of God, in the garden of love. [Author's emphasis]   3954-1

In addition to the quotes above, which hauntingly hint at the astounding concept that the stars are living entities, another example is found in the poem *Sparks* by an unknown author:

Surely in the future far
Man himself will be a star,
Shining by eternal light
Guiding pilgrims through the night.

Music of the Spheres

In the many references to stars contained his readings, Cayce frequently talked about them singing and the "music of the spheres." While this concept is apparently rooted in antiquity, it's best known from this famous Bible passage found in Job 38: 1–3: "Where were you when I laid the foundations of the Earth? Tell me, if you have understanding. Who laid the cornerstone, when the morning stars sang together, and all the sons of God shouted for joy?" A more recent example comes from the noted astronomer, astrologer, and mystic Johannes Kepler, who often talked about hearing the music of the spheres and who saw harmony in the movements of the planets in their orbits. (Regarded as one of the leading lights in the history of science for his formulation of the three laws of planetary motion that bear his name, Kepler, upon discovering them, excitedly exclaimed "O God, I am thinking Thy thoughts after Thee!" He obviously realized that he had tapped into the very mind of God itself in unveiling these fundamental secrets of the cosmos.)

Here now are just a few examples of the many passages found in the

Cayce readings about this celestial music:

> Then enter into meditation, in the wee hours of the morn-
> ing, when the world at large is quiet—when the music of
> the spheres and the morning stars sing for the glory of the
> coming day, and ask the soul; and let the spirit of self
> answer.   440-4

> In that before this, we find in the beginning, when the first
> of the elements were given, and the forces set in motion
> that brought about the sphere as we find called earth plane,
> and when the morning stars sang together . . .   294-8

> And as there was followed the receding of His Star, and the
> flight into Egypt through the devious ways and manners
> in which there came the news through word of mouth, yet
> in awe and quiet kept, it made for that in the experience of
> the entity—when it sits alone in the twilight, and there is
> almost again felt the music of the spheres, the singing of
> the morning stars, as the earth is quieted—there enters oft
> again that peace, that is only troubled by the cares of a
> workaday world.   1152-3

> This awoke within the entity that as may be found in the
> present, how all nature—the face in the water, the dew
> upon the grass, the tint and the beauty of the rose, the song
> of the stars, the mourn of the wind, all proclaim—*now*—
> the mighty words of a merciful, a loving God.   587-6

> Listen to the voice within, as it is awakened to the music of
> the spheres by the incoming of those forces that protect in
> those relationships through astronomical, astrological,
> and the influences as builded by self in its application of
> that known as *to* the relationships now.   539-2

In the experience there came that great overshadowing desire within the entity to become attuned, as it were, to the heavenly song, the heavenly music, the vibrations as it were of the spheres when all nature proclaimed the joyous event into the experience of man!   1487-1

Who may tell a rose to be sweet, or the music of the spheres to harmonize with God?   2408-1

In the present abilities we find the latent and manifested urge for the love of outdoors, of nature—as in voice, as in sound; whether the waves upon the seashore, the wind in the pines, the song of the birds, or the music as of nature and the spheres combined.   2450-1

Think, for a moment, of the music of the waves upon the shore, of the morning as it breaks with the music of nature, of the night as it falls with the hum of the insect, of all the kingdoms as they unite in their song of appreciation to an all-creative influence that gives nature consciousness or awareness of its being itself. And harmonize that in thine own appreciation, as to bring music akin to the song of the spheres.   2581-2

The name then was Melsanteudendt. The entity gained much, which is expressed at present in the interpretings of those things prompted by listening to the voice within, and of the activities of things pertaining to spiritual attitude—as the listening not only to the promptings from without but to the music of the spheres, or of the stars, or of nature itself.   2700-1

For the entity turned to nature, to nature's mysteries, to nature's beauty, to the songbirds, to flowers, to music of rain patter on the roof, as well as the music of the spheres for its inspiration.   3201-2

Faint not because of oppositions, but do keep the music of
the spheres, the light of the stars, the softness of the
moonlight upon the water as upon the trees. For nature in
its song, as the birds, as the bees make music to their
Creator, contributed to man   5265-1

The astronomical, the numerological, the environs of the
creations in the vibrations from metals, from stones, from
those of every form, have—through the experience of the
entity at times had their influence; and thus bear for the
entity something that must be used as an omen, or as an
experience that may aid the entity in making the proper
interpretations of those things that to many an one are not
lawful to be spoken in materiality—hence come only to
those who have eyes to see, through the spiritual realms, or
who have ears to hear the music of the spheres, the growing
or the beauty in all the relationships to man that make for
expressions of the divine that may be, and is, a portion of
man's experience.

No man, no physical matter, has ever seen *God* at any
time; only the *manifestations* of Him.   707-1

Such references to the music of the spheres and the stars singing to
us (however moving and lovely they may be) have for the most part
been taken only figuratively and as "poetic license." However all celestial objects—including the Sun, Moon, and planets of our solar system,
all of the stars, and even other galaxies, including our Milky Way—give
off radiation across the entire electromagnetic spectrum. And this includes not only ultraviolet, infrared (or heat), and visible light, but for
many of these bodies radio waves as well. The radio emissions themselves can be converted to sound waves, making it possible to actually
"listen" to the cosmos with our ears as well as look at it with our eyes.

Much of what is received for the most part sounds like static, hissing, or beeps (in the case of pulsars—spinning neutron stars). However, thanks to today's amazingly sensitive, huge radio telescopes, the incredible number-crunching capability of Cray supercomputers, and very sophisticated Moog electronic synthesizers, radio astronomers have found that some of the stars are emitting cyclic *harmonic* vibrations—not radio "noise" or random static—into space. This means that they in a sense *are* "singing" to us! Here, of course, we're talking about using giant "radio ears" and elaborate equipment to physically perceive it. But apparently it's possible to hear the celestial music without their use, for these modern marvels obviously didn't exist in Johannes Kepler's day— and yet he heard the music of the spheres! So did a number of the people for whom Edgar Cayce gave readings. In this regard, note especially what he had to say in some of the readings above concerning tuning into this music spiritually as well as physically. And just for the record here—I have had many people tell me at conferences where I was speaking that they have also heard the stars singing to them!

More About Stars

Before discussing entire families of suns, here are a few more of the author's favorite excerpts from the many psychic discourses by Edgar Cayce that mention stars:

> Who may tell the lily to represent beauty? Who may tell the violet to blush, even in the shady dell? Who may tell the stars or the sun and moon to worship God? The entity has seen, has found those things that answer within. Would that all would do likewise.   4065-1

> Who may tell the rose how to be beautiful? Who may tell the stars or the moon in its course how to raise in the heart and soul of man the longing to know the Creator of all? `
> 2600-2

> As the sun, the moon, the stars would be given for signs, for

seasons, for days, for years in man's experience—then it would not be amiss that these would indicate the symbols as they were represented in those stages or phases of experience in the earth.   288-50

Study also astrological subjects, not as termed by some, but rather in the light of that which may be gained through a study of His word. For, as it was given from the beginning, those planets, the stars, are given for signs, for seasons, for years, that man may indeed (in his contemplation of the universe) find his closer relationships. 5124-1

Train the entity in higher mathematics as will have to do with the electronics and dealing with the forces of the spheres. For the astronomy in the study of light, the study of the rays that are a part of each individual planet, each individual star, each individual asteroid are all a part of the forces in universal activities.   4081-1

He is the Alpha and Omega, the bright and morning star . . .
                                                          792-1

Hence we look out and see the heavens, the stars; and, as the psalmist has said: "The heavens declare the glory of God and the firmament sheweth his handiwork, as day unto day uttereth speech and night unto night sheweth knowledge."   262-56

Star Clusters: Stellar Jewelboxes and Beehives

As mentioned earlier in this chapter, stars are typically born into families ranging from double- and multiple-sun systems to much larger groupings known as star clusters. Cayce mentions the latter in one reading: " . . . when the priest then began to show the manifestations of those periods of reckoning the longitude (as termed now), latitude, and the activities of the planets and stars, and the various groups of stars, constellations, and the various influences that are held in place, or that *hold* in place those about this particular solar system." (294–150) It should be mentioned here that star clusters and constellations are two different types of celestial object; the former are gravitationally bound systems, moving through space together, while the latter with few exceptions are unassociated chance alignments of stars moving in different directions. Also, many well-known star patterns like the Big Dipper are not in themselves actually constellations, as widely believed, but rather are "asterisms." These are distinctive figures making up only a part of a constellation—in the case of the Big Dipper, Ursa Major, or the Great Bear.

Of the two basic types of star groupings, "open clusters" contain several hundred to more than a thousand members. And of this type undoubtedly the most famous of all is the magnificent Pleiades Star Cluster, more popularly know as the "Seven Sisters." It lies above the constellation Orion in the winter sky and appears as a misty little dipper-shaped cloud of stars to the unaided eye. Binoculars transform it into a wonder of the night, its stars appearing like blue-white sparkling diamonds against black velvet! (Incidentally, such glasses can reveal every major type of celestial object—ranging from the mountains, craters and valleys of our Moon, the four bright Galilean satellites of Jupiter, and comets to star clusters, nebulae, and even many of the brighter galaxies, including the majestic starclouds of our own Milky Way Galaxy.)

Edgar Cayce was certainly well aware of the Pleiades and mentioned it more than a dozen times in his readings (all within astrological contexts). In addition to that already given in 311-2 concerning Arcturus, here are a few of the more interesting references to this starry commune:

> In entering the earth's plane, we find the entity comes under the influence of Mercury, Jupiter, and of Mars, with the Pleiades and the Orion in the benevolent influence of the life.   5454-3

In taking the position in the present plane, we find the urges, and the manifest and latent, are from those of Jupiter, with Venus, Mercury, Mars, and of the Pleiades.

2698-1

In entering the earth's plane in the present life, we find the entity comes under the influences of Mercury, Jupiter, Mars, with the adverse influences of Venus and Saturn; the assistance in the influence of Uranus and of the Pleiades.

2675-4

In taking the position in the present earth's plane, we find under the influence of Jupiter and Venus, with Mercury and Uranus in the distance. In the adverse influence then of Vulcan and of the Pleiades.   569-6

In coming to the present earth plane, we find the entity taking its position from that of Venus, with those of the Pleiades, Jupiter and of Mercury, and with the benevolent influence of Saturn's forces in the degree that is seldom seen in the earth's plane. One with the adverse influence in Mars and in Vulcan's forces.   780-6

As these reading indicate, Cayce saw the astrological influence of the Pleiades as being mainly benevolent. This brings to mind Tennyson's famous lines about this lovely stellar jewelbox in his poem *Locksley Hall*:

> Many a night from yonder ivied casement,
> Ere I went to rest,
> Did I look on great Orion, sloping slowly
> to the west.
> Many a night I saw the Pleiads,
> rising thro' the mellow shade,
> Glitter like a swarm of fireflies
> tangled in a silver braid.

Also, note in the last two readings Edgar Cayce's reference to "Vulcan." This is the name astronomers centuries ago gave to a planet believed to lie in the same orbit as the Earth but on the opposite side of the Sun from us—and, therefore, which could never be seen from here. From many lines of evidence (including spacecraft that have actually been there!) we know that Vulcan doesn't exist. But here's what Cayce surprisingly had to say about this mythical planet:

> (Q) Is there a planet anciently known as Lilith or Vulcan?
> (A) Pluto and Vulcan are one and the same. No Lilith.
> Lilith is a personality.   826-8

What an amazing connection—given that Pluto itself wasn't discovered until 1930!

One other interesting fact concerning the Pleiades needs to be mentioned here. Many ancient cultures (especially Asian ones) claim that their ancestors came from this star cluster! This includes the Japanese, who have even named a car after it—the Subaru. The author has personally met a number of people in this country over the years who make the same claim. In fact, more than once following a lecture where I've set up my telescope and given those attending a view of the Pleiades, someone has burst into tears and said to me "That's my home!"

The second basic type of star grouping is that of the "globular clusters." These are enormous beehivelike swarms containing anywhere from 100,000 up to a million suns! Edgar Cayce didn't actually mention any of them by name as he did the Pleiades—probably because even the brightest of them are only barely visible without optical aid, due to their great distances from us. But I truly hope he may have had the opportunity of seeing one of these starballs through a large telescope. The incredible spectacle greeting the eye of hundreds of thousands of remote suns staring back at you is quite beyond any words to describe! And we can only imagine what the night sky must look like to anyone living on a planet within such a cluster. (This is, in fact, the basis for Isaac Asimov's *Nightfall*—one of the greatest science fiction short stories ever written. Based upon the immortal lines in one of Emerson's essays—"If the stars should appear one night in a thousand years . . . "—it's a story about a planet that has multiple suns in its sky, causing it to become dark only once in several centuries. When it does, its inhabitants find themselves living inside of an immense globular cluster with countless numbers of blazing stars shining in their heavens like a starry blizzard!

In the author's opinion, the ultimate reference to stars and clusters of stars (and all things celestial!) is the late Carl Sagan's classic work *Cosmos* (Random House, 1980) and the visually stunning thirteen–part PBS television series based upon it. Both the book itself and a 2005 version of the video presentation, updated by Sagan's wife and noted writer Ann Druyan, are available from the PBS Web site at pbs.org. It's estimated that at least one–fifth of the human race—well over a billion people—have watched *Cosmos!* Sagan truly was an eloquent spokesman for planet Earth and for the universe itself. As such, he is sorely missed. But he is at home among the stars he so loved.

---

[2]The word *galaxy* does appear in one reading: "(Q) The 'Primitive Man in Light' looked out from the earth and saw us within the sphere of the Universe with its constellations which combined to form his consciousness. He knew then, that a 'Way of Escape' from the rounds of Reincarnation opened beyond this Universe–beyond the Galaxy–beyond the opening in the forehead of Cepheus. Will you explain this 'Way of Escape'?"

"(A) We do not find it so. For we have this: These are the basis of–Let's get what is the first principle here. These are concepts, these are not the activities of individuals who look out upon that; not as the earth as the center of its activities, but as the own solar system, here. It is true that the activities so far as in this sphere or Galaxy of activities of the planetary forces within this present solar system, the earth first became as the indwelling of the consciousness of the race or the man in this particular sphere . . . " (1602-3) Here it appears that the word *galaxy* refers to our own Milky Way Galaxy.

[3]Galaxies used to be known as "island universes"–a term that Edgar Cayce may well have been familiar with, as it was widely used in his day.

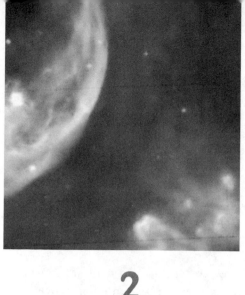

2

Life Elsewhere in the Universe

ARE WE ALONE?

One of the most hauntingly profound questions in all of science (as well as religion and philosophy) is whether or not we are alone in this vast universe. And as the noted physicist Lee DuBridge put it, "Either alternative is mind-boggling." For if we are not alone—if we have sisters and brothers living on other worlds—it means there are other sentient beings "out there" with whom we may someday (or may already have, according to some) come into contact. But if we are alone—if we are the only living intelligent entities in all the cosmos—it brings with it both a realization of how unique and privileged we are and a deep responsibility to preserve that life as unbelievably precious. The writer Thomas Carlyle cynically summed up the issue of life on other worlds as follows: "A sad spectacle. If they be inhabited, what a scope for misery and folly. If they be not inhabited, what a waste of space."!

But most of us who are absolutely convinced from the massive evi-

19

dence of both science and basic logic that we cannot possibly be alone in the cosmos take a much more optimistic approach to this momentous subject. Here are just a few of the reasons for our conviction:

- There are more stars (other suns) within reach of our largest telescopes today than *all the grains of sand on all the beaches and deserts on the entire planet Earth*! Galaxies can host as many as a trillion stars. And there are an estimated 100 billion galaxies within the currently observable universe.
- We now know that most if not all stars have planets orbiting them. This is solidly based upon both theoretical and observational grounds.
- All the essential building blocks for life are scattered profusely throughout interstellar space and on countless other worlds. This includes vast amounts of water itself, which is found in the frozen, liquid, and vapor states—which, in the last instance, includes the outer atmospheres of relatively cool red–giant and supergiant stars as steam.
- We ourselves are literally made of stardust, for the elements in our bodies were fused inside of exploding stars eons ago. We are children of the stars!
- We seemed to have been genetically programmed to return to our source—to venture into that cosmos from which we sprang and join that galactic community of which we surely are a part. As the philosopher Eric Hoffer expressed it, "It's a kind of homing impulse—we are drawn to where we came from."

The beloved anthropologist and philosopher Loren Eiseley tells us in *The Immense Journey* that "So deep is the conviction that there must be life out there beyond the dark, one thinks that if they are more advanced than ourselves they may come across space at any moment, perhaps in our generation." And in a similar vein, Sir Arthur Clarke's classic science fiction short story *The Sentinel* (the basis for the famous movie *2001: A Space Odyssey*) contains the following lines: "I can never look now at the Milky Way without wondering from which of those banked clouds of stars the emissaries are coming. If you will pardon so commonplace a simile, we have set off the fire–alarm and have nothing to do but to wait. I do not think we will have to wait for long." This remark refers to the fictional beacon set up by aliens that was triggered upon our reaching the Moon. But, in fact, the human race has long been inadvertently letting others know of our presence through radio and television broadcasts that leak out into space. (There has also been at least one enormously powerful message intentionally beamed to the stars from the huge 1,000–foot diameter radio telescope in Arecibo, Puerto Rico.)

One of NASA's former associate administrators, Wesley Huntress, has stated: "We used to think that life was fragile. But wherever liquid water and chemical energy are found, there is life. There is no exception. Life may be a cosmic imperative." And it may well go far beyond this, for there's a growing suspicion among many researchers that *the universe itself is alive*! As the radio astronomer Gerrit Verschuur expressed it, "We must think seriously about relocating the dividing line between living and non–living organisms. I no longer believe that it is at the edge of the body's epidermis or at the edge of the atmosphere. It is at the edge of the Universe."

In his superb fictional novel *The Black Cloud*, the late British cosmologist Sir Fred Hoyle wrote one of the most brilliant and amazing accounts of such a possibility. As one of the very few works of science fiction that ever ended up actually being reviewed in the various astronomical periodicals, it's so technically sound and convincingly written that many astronomers (including the author) believe Hoyle was attempting to share something he knew to be so sensational yet true through the safe medium of fiction. Many other famous names have also been thought to have done the same, including the late astronomer Dr. Carl Sagan in his novel and movie *Contact*, and Sir Arthur Clarke himself (particularly in his short story *The Sentinel* mentioned above).

But it's not just scientists that suspect this. Visionaries and poets have also frequently hinted at such a profound possibility. Among them, Harry Elmore Hurd opened his haunting poem *The Irreducible Minimum* with the lines "Wonder of wonder, here am I, sentient to Earth and sea and star;" and concluded it by saying that we " . . . guess, although we cannot know, that Earth and stars and men are all one." That was back in 1944. At the rapidly accelerating pace of modern astronomical, astrophysical, and astrobiological research, we may well know if this exciting concept is indeed true within our lifetimes. If proven to be so, the implications and ramifications for humanity will be utterly mind–blowing!

Cayce and Extraterrestrials

Given all of the above, what did Edgar Cayce himself have to say about life on other planets? While today's popular terms "extraterrestrials," "extraterrestrial life," and "aliens" (this last in the context of other life forms) do not appear in any of the Cayce material, he did comment on this subject in several readings found under the search headings of "life in space," "life on other worlds," and "other worlds." His negative response in two of these is often quoted when this topic comes up among ET skeptics. But as we'll see, these must be taken in context. And in the others he does indeed indicate that there *are* other beings in the universe! (In fact, one reading contains a reference to other civilizations that's nothing short of amazing for all of us who believe in or recognize Christ.) Here are the corresponding readings:

> (Q) Are any of the planets, other than the earth, inhabited
> by human beings or animal life of any kind?
> (A) No.   3744-4

> (Q) Upon what planets other than the earth does human
> life exist?
> (A) None as human life in the earth. This has just been
> given.   826-8

> For, much might be given respecting those environs and as
> to how or why there have been and are accredited to the
> various planets certain characterizations that make for the
> attractions of souls' sojourns in that environ. But these are

places of abode. As in the earth we find the elements are peopled, as the earth has its own moon or satellites enjoined in its environ, so is it with the other planets. The earth with its three-fourths water, with its elements, is peopled; yes. So are the various activities in other solar systems.   541-1

The entity was among the priestesses of the Mayan experience. It was just before that period when those as from the east had come, and there were the beginnings of the unfoldments of the understanding that there were other portions of the same land, or those that were visiting from other worlds or planets. [GD's note: Psychic experiences of prehistory? Space Ships, flying saucers?]   1616-1
      (Bracketed remarks are often by the stenographer of the reading; in this case, Gladys Davis.)

Man may become, with the people of the universe, ruler of any of the various spheres through which the soul passes in its experiences.   281-16

It's important to recognize in the first two readings that it is the planets of our own solar system that were being discussed. While those about other stars were speculated about in Cayce's time, it's only in the past two decades that they have been proven to actually exist and have become accepted as commonplace by the general public. So in these readings concerning life on other planets (as well as planetary sojourns), he was being asked about the familiar nine primary worlds of our own solar system. (Officially it's now only eight since the demotion of poor Pluto to the status of a "dwarf planet" by the International Astronomical Union in 2006!) And modern research from both ground-based and orbiting telescopes, and especially from flybys of these worlds by spacecraft, certainly supports the fact that there are no others like us on the various planets of our solar system. There may well be aquatic life forms on the satellites of several of them that have ice-covered liquid water

oceans, like Europa, or microbial life under the surface of Mars, or organisms floating in the atmospheres of one of the four gas giants, like
Jupiter. But the Earth is the only body that can support humanoid life
as we know it.

However, in the third reading, Edgar Cayce did speak about *other solar
systems* as actual abodes of life—about their planets being "peopled"—
and in the fourth reading he even talked about visits by beings from
other worlds! The fifth reading actually refers to "people of the universe," clearly implying that life exists throughout the cosmos. In these
readings he was surely correct, for there is now very solid evidence that
at least one planet in each solar system will lie within the so-called
"zone of habitability" of its sun, where liquid water can exist and life-
giving "solar" energy is plentiful. Had he been asked about the existence of physical beings on the planets orbiting some of our bright stellar
neighbors—about their presence in the case of such well-known stars
as Vega or Arcturus or Capella or Betelgeuse—his response might well
have been most enlightening. But sadly, no one at that time thought to
ask such a question!

A Cosmic Christ

So the Cayce readings on this subject (relatively limited in number as
they are) do not rule out the existence of life elsewhere in the universe,
but rather they accommodate and support the growing awareness that
we are certainly not alone in this vast cosmos. And there's still at least
one other fascinating reading by Edgar Cayce that not only allows for
the possibility that other worlds are populated—but strongly implies
that they indeed *are* inhabited! We find this amazing statement: "Not
the Christ, but His messenger, with the Christ from the beginning, and is
to other worlds what the Christ is to this earth." (262-71) The implication
is that the Christ Spirit has enlightened many other civilizations
throughout the long history of the universe. As the poet Alice Meynell
so beautifully expressed it in these lines taken from her 1913 poem
Christ in the Universe:

Nor, in our little day,
May His devices with the heavens be guessed
His pilgrimage to thread the Milky Way
Or his bestowals there, be manifest.
But in the eternities,
Doubtless we shall compare together, hear
A million alien gospels, in what guise
He trod the Pleiades, the Lyre, the Bear.
O be prepared my soul!
To read the inconceivable, to scan
The million forms of God those stars unroll
When, in our turn, we show to them a man.

In mentioning Christ, two well-known Bible verses have always seemed to the author as inferences about other planets and other beings. In John 10:16 we are told, "And other sheep I have which are not of this fold." While generally taken to mean those outside of the faith, in a larger context Christ may well have been referring to those other worlds that His Father has created and populated. The other verse is "In my Father's house are many mansions," found in John 14:2. To my mind as an astronomer, "mansions" (sometimes translated as "rooms") is a reference to other planets and "house" to the very universe itself!

Alternative Life Forms

When considering the existence of life elsewhere in the cosmos as we have so far in this chapter, the assumption is usually made that it's life in a physical form that's being discussed. But as Sir Fred Hoyle suggested in his novel *The Black Cloud*, mentioned above, it may also be found in the form of beings without bodies—ones consisting of pure thought and energy. Interestingly, Edgar Cayce talked in a number of his readings about highly evolved "energy beings" consisting of individualized "thought forms" without physical bodies that came to our planet millions of years ago. Through a process known as "involution," they pushed or infused their consciousness into the matter and primitive life forms existing on the Earth at that time. Here are a few of those readings pertaining to such entities:

> ... there came first those in the earth as thought forms that were able to partake of that about them; and so absorb them, much as we see in the lower forms of material manifestations in life, and *moved* by the spirit to become that they found or absorbed in their being.   5756-11

> Hence as we find, when souls sought or found manifestation in materiality by the projection of themselves into matter—as became thought forms—and when this had so enticed the companions or souls of the Creator, first we had then the creation in which "God breathed into man (God-made) the breath of life and he became a living soul," with the abilities to become godlike.   257-201

> As has been indicated through other associations, the influences of those souls that sought material expression pushed themselves into thought forms in the earth. And owing to the earth's relative position with the activities in this particular sphere of activity in the universe, it was chosen as the place for expression.   262-119

> As to their forms in the physical sense, these were much *rather* of the nature of *thought forms,* or able to push out *of themselves* in that direction in which its development took shape in thought—much in the way and manner as the amoeba would in the waters of a stagnant bay, or lake, in the present.   364-3

> From that which has been given, it is seen that individuals in the beginning were more of thought forms than individual entities with personalities as seen in the present, and their projections into the realms of fields of thought

that pertain to a developing or evolving world of matter, with the varied presentations about same, of the expressions or attributes in the various things about the entity or individual, or body, through which such science—as termed now, or such phenomena as would be termed—became manifest. Hence we find occult or psychic science, as would be called at the present, was rather the natural state of man in the beginning   364-10

Before that we find the entity was in the land now thought of or termed as La, or Mu—Lamu.
    Those experiences then made for the determining between the thought forms and those that materialized into what became man.   1387-1

Before that the entity was also in the Atlantean land, when there were the first of the destructive forces applied in the attempts to bring individuals into the better associations, where there were the lesser developments (those individuals who were partly thought-forms).   2031-1

In the February 2002 issue of *Personal Spirituality*, one of the A.R.E's newsletters, John Van Auken tells us that the ancient Egyptians referred to humankind as "godlings" and considered the souls to be stars in the heavens of God's mind. He expands on this theme so beautifully and eloquently that the author simply must share it in John's own words:

"According to this legend, on that first morning, flush with life—our young minds ablaze with wonder—we godlings began to explore the Cosmos. As children do, we peered into the many mansions of our Father's house and found wonders upon wonders. Eventually, some of us came to this present solar system, with its beautiful star and nine planets. Our first appearance here was not an incarnation, per se, because there were no human bodies then. In that dawn, we were *minds* in the breeze, *voices* in the wind—voices foretelling of the eventual coming of humanity. With a youthful joy, we looked forward to entering this new realm and exploring its wonders.

Earth was not the only planet we visited, nor was the third dimension our primary level of consciousness. The universe was ours to enjoy. By doing so, we would grow to become true companions to the Creator of the universe, who loves us and longs to enjoy our companionship. In quiet moments we may sense the truth of this story . . . How have we lost touch with this truth? How have we become so terrestrial, so temporary? Where is our celestial, eternal nature, our mind that once flew through the Cosmos? Cayce says that it is still within us waiting to be awakened!"

The point of all this is that, here again, the Cayce readings suggest that life has long existed elsewhere in the universe. The fact that it may not take on the form of physical bodies like ours makes it no less real. Indeed, many visionaries and futurists see the ultimate end result of the human evolutionary process as just that—of our existing as pure thought and spiritual energy! Those readers who are longtime *Star Trek* fans will recognize this as a recurring theme in many of its stories (especially in the original series).

Going Deeper

The lure of extraterrestrial life is so exciting and compelling that countless books (both on a scholarly and a popular level), movies, television documentaries, magazine articles, and research papers exist on the subject. (There have also been many national and international scientific conferences devoted to it.) Below are just a few of the author's favorites among these. Most of the books themselves are out-of-print but still widely available in libraries and used-book stores. Fictional accounts dominate this selection, as they convey in a way that no academic work possibly can the heady excitement of making contact with other beings from out there among the stars.

- *Intelligent Life in the Universe*, I.S. Shklovskii and Carl Sagan, Holden-Day/Dell, 1966 (factual book)
- *We Are Not Alone*, Walter Sullivan, McGraw–Hill/Dell Publishing, 1964 (factual book)
- *Contact*, Carl Sagan, Pocket Books/Warner Brothers, 1985/1997 (fictional book and movie; screenplay coauthored by Sagan's wife Ann Druyan)
- *The Listeners*, James Gunn, Ballantine Books/Del Rey, 1972 (fictional book)
- *The Black Cloud*, Sir Fred Hoyle, Harper & Row/Signet, 1957 (fictional book)
- *The Day the Earth Stood Still*, Harry Bates/screenplay by Edmund North, Twentieth Century Fox, 1951, (all–time classic fictional movie)
- *2001: A Space Odyssey*, Sir Arthur Clarke/Stanley Kubrick, Del Rey/Warner Brothers, 1968 (fictional book and movie)
- *Close Encounters of the Third Kind*, Steven Spielberg, Dell/Columbia Pictures, 1977/1980 (factual book and fictional movie—based on the book by J. Allen Hynek)

An Internet search will turn up literally thousands of "hits" for those desiring to explore this momentous field in depth. And before taking leave here of the subject of life elsewhere in the universe, it should be mentioned that yet another much more esoteric aspect of life existing "out there" in the cosmos—one intimately involving each of us personally—lies ahead in the heady discussions to be found in a later chapter!

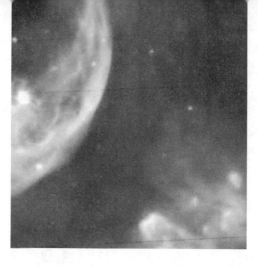

3

Earth Changes and Cosmic Cataclysms

POLE SHIFT AND PHYSICAL CHANGES

The one subject that seems to captivate students of the Cayce material perhaps more than any other concerns his readings about coming Earth changes. He divided these into two major types: physical changes and mental changes. And while the latter are certainly extremely important and tied hand–in–hand with the former, it's the actual predicted physical changes to our planet already underway that is the focus of this chapter.

Atmospheric, oceanic, seismic, and geological changes/upheavals are all to be found in the Cayce readings. Let's begin here with what has to be the most ominous of any of these and what would assuredly be the ultimate disaster of all—that known as "pole shift," or the movement of our planet's geographic poles of rotation in space. There's no question that the Earth's magnetic poles have shifted and reversed repeatedly in the past and, in fact, are in the process of slowly beginning to do so again right now. But there's also evidence that our planet has actually shifted *physically* on its axis to varying degrees as well over its long history.

If this surprises you, I should point out that this is something that has also happened on other planets in our solar system. We know, for example, that Venus is "upside down" and rotating backwards (clockwise as seen from above the planet) with respect to the counterclockwise rotation of most of these worlds including the Earth. There's also evidence that the poles of Mars were once where its equator currently is located. And perhaps most amazing of all, the planet Uranus—nearly four times the size of the Earth—is tilted over 98 degrees and rotates lying on its side! So worlds definitely can and do move on their axes. Let's look then at those Cayce readings specifically mentioning the shifting of our planet's poles:

> (Q) What will be the type and extent of the upheaval in '36?
> (A) The wars, the upheavals in the interior of the earth, and the shifting of same by the differentiation in the axis as respecting the positions from the Polaris center (the Pole Star).   5748-6

> These will not come [political changes in Italy], as we find, as broken, before the catastrophes of outside forces to the earth in '36, which will come from the shifting of the equilibrium of the earth itself in space, with those of the consequential effects upon the various portions of the country—or world—affected by same.   3976-10

> The entity then was among those who were of that group who gathered to rid the earth of the enormous animals which overran the earth, but ice, the entity found, nature, God, changed the poles and the animals were destroyed, though man attempted it in that activity of the meetings.
>   5249-1

> (Q) What great change or the beginning of what change, if

any, is to take place in the earth in the year 2000 to 2001
A.D.?
(A) When there is a shifting of the poles. Or a new cycle
begins.   826-8

As to the changes physical again: The earth will be broken
up in the western portion of America. The greater portion
of Japan must go into the sea. The upper portion of Europe
will be changed as in the twinkling of an eye. Land will
appear off the east coast of America. There will be the
upheavals in the Arctic and in the Antarctic that will make
for the eruption of volcanos in the Torrid areas, and there
will be shifting then of the poles—so that where there has
been those of a frigid or the semi-tropical will become the
more tropical, and moss and fern will grow. And these will
begin in those periods in '58 to '98, when these will be
proclaimed as the periods when His light will be seen again
in the clouds. As to times, as to seasons, as to places, *alone*
is it given to those who have named the name—and who
bear the mark of those of His calling and His election in
their bodies. To them it shall be given . . .
(Q) What are the world changes to come this year [1934]
physically?
(A) The earth will be broken up in many places. The early
portion will see a change in the physical aspect of the west
coast of America. There will be open waters appear in the
northern portions of Greenland. There will be new lands
seen off the Caribbean Sea, and *dry* land will appear.
                                                        3976-15

Before this we find the entity in that land now known as the
American, during the periods when the *Lemurian* or the
lands of Mu or Zu were being in their turmoils for destruction.
    And the entity was among those that—in what is now

not far from that land in which the entity in this sojourn
first saw the light—(that must in the near future fade again
into those joinings with the land of Mu)—established a
temple of worship for those that escaped from the turmoils
of the shifting of the earth at that particular period.

509-1

In the record chambers there were more ceremonies than
in calling the peoples at the finishing of that called the
pyramid. For, here those that were trained in the Temple
of Sacrifice as well as in the Temple Beautiful were about
the sealing of the record chambers. For, these were to be
kept as had been given by the priests in *Atlantis* or Poseidia
(Temple), when these records of the race, of the developments, of the laws pertaining to one were put in their
chambers and to be opened only when there was the
returning of those into materiality, or to earth's experience, when the change was imminent in the earth; which
change, we see, begins in '58 and ends with the changes
wrought in the upheavals and the shifting of the poles, as
begins then the reign in '98 (as time is counted in the
present) of those influences that have been given by many
in the records that have been kept by those sojourners in
this land of the Semitic peoples.   378-16

Mental Changes

While we're not focusing on the mental changes that Edgar Cayce
mentioned in connection with Earth changes in this book, this would
seem to be a good place before moving on to share at least something
of what he saw in this regard since it occurs within the text of a reading
quoted above.

As to those things that deal with the mental of the earth,
these shall call upon the mountains to cover many. As ye

have seen those in lowly places raised to those of power in the political, in the machinery of nations' activities, so shall ye see those in high places reduced and calling on the waters of darkness to cover them. And those that in the inmost recesses of their selves awaken to the spiritual truths that are to be given, and those places that have acted in the capacity of teachers among men, the rottenness of those that have ministered in places will be brought to light, and turmoils and strifes shall enter. And, as there is the wavering of those that would enter as emissaries, as teachers, from the throne of life, the throne of light, the throne of immortality, and wage war in the air with those of darkness, then know ye the Armageddon is at hand. For with the great numbers of the gathering of the hosts of those that have hindered and would make for man and his weaknesses stumbling blocks, they shall wage war with the spirits of light that come into the earth for this awakening; that have been and are being called by those of the sons of men into the service of the living God. For He, as ye have been told, is not the God of the dead, not the God of those that have forsaken Him, but those that love His coming, that love His associations among men—the God of the *living*, the God of Life! For, He *is* Life.   3976-15

There are two important things to note concerning the dates mentioned by Cayce in several of the above readings. First, psychics are often correct in their predictions of events but frequently off in the times given for their occurrence. Secondly, while these dates have all come and gone, the changes within the body of the Earth itself leading up to a shift of its axis may have actually started during the specified times. And in fact, the words "begin," "begins" and "beginning" all appear in some of those readings. I, for one, am convinced that what Edgar Cayce saw will sooner or later come to pass. And many Native Americans are convinced, too, seeing this as the inevitable "cleansing" of planet Earth and the time of the "great purification." It will, also, of necessity in order to survive be that time when humanity will have to take leave of our beautiful "Spaceship Earth" (as philosopher and visionary Buckminster Fuller called it) and venture into the awaiting cosmos. Many refer to this transition as "graduation day" for our race.

Earthquakes and Tsunamis

Among other types of physical Earth changes are earthquakes both on land and beneath the oceans. One of the most hauntingly accurate predictions concerns the recent quake and resulting horrific tsunami that happened in the Indian Ocean on December 26, 2004—killing at least 200,000 people and leaving millions homeless and helpless. We're told in one reading:

> **Strifes will arise through the period. Watch for them near Davis Strait in the attempts there for the keeping of the life line to a land open. Watch for them in Libya and in *Egypt*, in Ankara and in Syria, through the straits about those areas above Australia, in the Indian Ocean and the *Persian* Gulf.**
>
> **Ye say that these are of the sea; yes—for there shall the breaking up be, until there are those in every land that shall say that this or that shows the hand of divine interference, or that it is nature taking a hand, or that it is the natural consequence of good judgments.   3976-2**

How uncannily prophetic—and tragically true.

Changes in Sea Level and Geography

A fascinating glimpse into the future involving changes in the sea level and coastlines of the United States appears to have been given to Edgar Cayce in a dream—as described in the following question put to him at the Fifth Annual Congress of the A.R.E. held in Virginia Beach in June of 1936:

(Q) Interpret and explain the *dream* which Edgar Cayce [had] on March 3, 1936, in which he was born again over two hundred years in the future and traveled to various sections of this country where records of Edgar Cayce could be found. [Dream was as follows:]

(A) I had been born again in 2158 A.D. in Nebraska. The sea apparently covered all of the western part of the country, as the city where I lived was on the coast. The family name was a strange one. At an early age as a child I declared myself to be Edgar Cayce who had lived 200 years before. Scientists, men with long beards, little hair, and thick glasses, were called in to observe me. They decided to visit the places where I said I had been born, lived and worked, in Kentucky, Alabama, New York, Michigan, and Virginia. Taking me with them the group of scientists visited these places in a long, cigar-shaped, metal flying ship which moved at high speed. Water covered part of Alabama. Norfolk, Virginia, had become an immense seaport. New York [City] had been destroyed either by war or an earthquake and was being rebuilt. Industries were scattered over the countryside. Most of the houses were of glass. Many records of my work as Edgar Cayce were discovered and collected. The group returned to Nebraska, taking the records with them to study.   294-185

Perhaps Edgar Cayce's most extensive and explicit discourse about coming changes in the geography of this country, resulting from rising sea levels, as well as preparation for these changes came to him in one of his psychic readings rather than in a dream:

As to conditions in the geography of the world, of the country—changes here are gradually coming about.

No wonder, then, that the entity feels the need, the necessity for change of central location.

For, many portions of the east coast will be disturbed,

as well as many portions of the west coast, as well as the central portion of the U.S.

In the next few years lands will appear in the Atlantic as well as in the Pacific. And what is the coast line now of many a land will be the bed of the ocean. Even many of the battle fields of the present will be ocean, will be the seas, the bays, the lands over which the *new* order will carry on their trade as one with another.

Portions of the now east coast of New York, or New York City itself, will in the main disappear. This will be another generation, though, here; while the southern portions of Carolina, Georgia—these will disappear. This will be much sooner.

The waters of the lakes will empty into the Gulf, rather than the waterway over which such discussions have been recently made. It would be well if the waterways were prepared, but not for that purpose for which it is at present being considered.

Then the area where the entity is now located [Virginia Beach for reading] will be among the safety lands, as will be portions of what is now Ohio, Indiana and Illinois, and much of the southern portion of Canada and the eastern portion of Canada; while the western land—much of that is to be disturbed—in this land—as, of course, much in other lands.

Then, with the knowledge of these—first the principles, then the material changes.

The choice should be made by the entity itself as to location, and especially as to the active work.

To be *sure* there is work to be done by the entity, *definite* work.

Join with all of those who declare that the Lord has come and that His day is again at hand.

Ready for questions.

(Q) Should this work start by early fall?

(A) Start today!

(Q) I have for many months felt that I should move away from New York City.

(A) This is well, as indicated. There is too much unrest; there will continue to be the character of vibrations that to the body will be disturbing, and eventually those destructive forces there—though these will be in the next generation.

(Q) Will Los Angeles be safe?

(A) Los Angeles, San Francisco, most all of these will be among those that will be destroyed before New York even.

(Q) Should California or Virginia Beach be considered at all, or where is the right place that God has already provided for me to live?

(A) As indicated, these choices should be made rather in self. Virginia Beach or the area is much safer as a definite place. But the work of the entity should embrace most all of the areas from the east to the west coast, in its persuading—not as a preacher, nor as one bringing a message of doom, but as a loving warning to all groups, clubs, woman's clubs, writer's clubs, art groups, those of every form of club, that there needs be—in their activities—definite work towards the knowledge of the power of the Son of God's activity in the affairs of men.

(Q) Are there special groups with which I should become affiliated, in doing the work that God is urging His people to do now, impersonally?

(A) Rather as indicated, use that wherein there is the likeness, see? Magnify those things that are the virtues in all, minimizing the faults that are there. Not as a member of a group. May be member of an organization, but rather than as a member of a group be a helpmeet to *all* groups! As just indicated, clubs of every nature.

Arouse them to *their* abilities; by writing as well as speaking. For the entity has the abilities in these directions, as has been indicated . . .

(Q) Should I have a real home again?

(A) Have a real home, or where it would be as headquarters—where the entity would spend most of its time when
not *actually* engaged in assisting various groups in portions of the country . . .

Each of these have various centers, various groups that are
making studies. During portions of the seasons when
these are most active—in the winter be in the South and
the West and the Southwest. In the spring be in the central
portions. And in the summer in Maine, in California, in
Washington state, in Ohio—in the various portions of the
land, see? But some place—as Virginia Beach or Norfolk
or environs, or Richmond—as home.

(Q) Is Virginia Beach to be safe?

(A) It is the center—and the only seaport and center—of
the White Brotherhood.   1152-11

This exchange certainly makes it clear why the readings urged Edgar
Cayce to choose Virginia Beach for his center—it is without question a
very significant and special place.

Before continuing, I must share a little-known fact that certainly con-
firms this. A total eclipse of the Sun is perhaps nature's grandest spectacle. As the Moon covers the Sun during the precious few minutes of
totality, our Daytime Star's pearly corona and crimson prominences
become visible, day turns to night, the stars come out, and the temperature typically falls as much as thirty degrees! It's also an extremely rare
event in terms of seeing it from any given location, centuries passing
before repeat performances. And even then, the path of the Moon's
shadow cast onto the Earth by the eclipsed Sun is a narrow cone aver-
aging only a hundred miles or so across—and you *must* be within it to
see the eclipse as total. On March 7, 1970, a total eclipse of the Sun
occurred over Virginia Beach. As I and countless others watched from
the beach, the Moon's shadow swept across us and *right over the A.R.E.
complex*. Yes—a very special place indeed!

It should be mentioned here that *global warming* is a major contributor to the rising sea levels, as more and more glaciers are melting, and the ice sheets are retreating in both the Arctic and the Antarctic. There's no longer any doubt that such a warm–up of our planet is really happening. (As just one example of the impact global warming is having—one that sounds like something right out of the above readings—British Prime Minister Tony Blair was told by his science advisors that the coastline maps of their country would need to be redrawn within the next ten years due to the rising sea levels!)

Asteroid and Comet Impacts

Although a pole shift itself is certainly a cataclysm of true cosmic proportions, there are other cataclysmic events that can and have befallen our planet from space itself. I'm referring to the ongoing bombardment of the Earth (and its neighbor, the Moon) by meteors, asteroids, and comets. There's absolutely no doubt that at least the last two types of astronomical bodies have caused mass extinctions of life—as well as major atmospheric, oceanic, geologic, and geographic upheavals—on our planet for billions of years now. In the case of comets, they may have also spawned life here in addition to taking it, for it's now widely believed by scientists that these carbon–rich "dirty snowballs" were not only the major source of our oceans but that they also seeded them with organic molecules—the precursors of life!

One night in April of 2001, a mile–long asteroid—made of solid iron and rock and traveling at more than 40,000 miles an hour—passed between the Moon and the Earth in a near miss. Just a few weeks before Christmas of 2005, one of these hurtling projectiles came *ten times closer to us than the Moon!* And this has happened repeatedly throughout history. It's known for certain that this is what took out the dinosaurs some sixty–five million years ago—the actual impact crater having been found on and around the Yucatan Peninsula, half underground and half underwater. (By the way, most of the dinosaurs were not killed by the impact itself but rather by the dense cloud of debris that was thrown into the atmosphere and that hid the Sun for perhaps a year or more.

Being largely vegetarians, the dinosaurs starved to death without sunlight to feed the plant life.) There's now strong evidence that the "great extinction" that resulted from the breaking apart of the supercontinent Gowanaland was also caused by an impact from an enormous asteroid or huge comet nucleus rather than by plate tectonics, as was widely believed.

As many respected experts in this field have emphatically stated, it's not a question of *if* a major impact is going to happen again but *when*. There are now a number of heavily supported government programs worldwide dedicated to identifying potential threatening bodies, including Near-Earth Asteroids (NEAs) which pose the greatest risk to us. It's widely agreed that a major impact could spell the end of our civilization. But if we're to take Edgar Cayce's silence about such cosmic cataclysms as any indication, apparently this isn't really going to happen. Quite surprisingly (especially in view of the above facts, at least some of which he was undoubtedly aware of), there's absolutely nothing in his Earth changes readings or any others about the impact of such bodies and the devastation of our planet! (Cayce didn't mention comets at all and asteroids only once.) Perhaps the various plans now on the drawing boards to deflect or destroy such objects before they hit us will succeed. Let's hope that they do!

The Missing Planet

While Edgar Cayce said nothing about the destruction of Earth by an asteroid, he did apparently refer to the destruction of the planet from which the asteroids themselves are believed to have originated! Between the orbits of Mars and Jupiter lies a vast field of cosmic rubble known as the Asteroid Zone or Belt. More than 10,000 objects have been catalogued there by astronomers, ranging in size from 600-mile-diameter Ceres (the largest body in the zone) to boulder-sized chunks. There's a fascinating relationship known as "Bode's Law" that gives the distances of the various planets from the Sun, with that of the Earth being taken as 1.0 At 1.5 we find Mars and at 5.2 Jupiter. According to this law, there should be a planet at 2.8 times the Earth's distance—but there is none. Instead we find the asteroids. It's long been believed that there was, in fact, once a planet there and that some cosmic cataclysm destroyed it, leaving behind the asteroids we find today.

The following remarkable statement appears in reading 195–43: "For this, as is seen, will be proven, that, as the scientific change has been found by the observation into the terrestrial forces and into those places and conditions about the earth's plane, *there is missing some one of the earth's companions or planets, and the combustion or destruction of same caused much changes*, see?" (Author's emphasis.) Here again is a superb but little-known example of Edgar Cayce's unprecedented psychic powers pertaining to the cosmos. It goes without saying that as an astronomer, I'm absolutely amazed at his profound insights about things celestial!

In addition to the Cayce readings themselves, a vast body of literature exists on the subject of this chapter, both technical and popular in content. For those desiring to explore more about this vital topic, among the most readable and fascinating of these works are the following books:

- *Pole Shift*, John White, July 1985.
- *Coming Earth Changes*, William Hutton, September 1996.
- *Edgar Cayce's Predictions for the 21st Century*, Mark Thurston, May 2005.

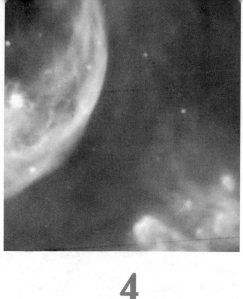

4

Other Universes and Dimensions

BUBBLE UNIVERSES

The words "universe" and "universal forces" are each mentioned some 1,500 times in the Cayce readings. These are mainly used in the opening of many of his readings, a common example being "Yes, we have the entity here, and those relations with the universe and universal forces, as are latent and exhibited in the present entity." But not only is "universe" used in the singular in other places and contexts, it's also spoken of in the plural—as "universes" and "other universes." They are mentioned in the following readings directly in some cases and as implied in others:

> For, remember, all of these planets, stars, universes, were made for the *entity* and its associates to rule, and not be ruled by them—save as an individual entity gives itself to their influences.
> 2830-2

Thus in the answers we may find that, though there may be
worlds, many universes, even much as to solar systems,
greater than our own that we enjoy in the present, this
earthly experience on this earth is a mere speck when
considered even with our own solar system. Yet the soul of
man, thy soul, encompasses *all* in this solar system or in
others.   5755-2

As it views itself into the worlds about itself, it recognizes
not only that it is a part of this material manifestation of
individual entities but a part of a universal consciousness
of *worlds* apparently without end.   1776-1

For, the earth is only an atom in the universe of *worlds!*
                                                           5749-3

This is absolutely astounding, for there's now both theoretical and
observational evidence that what we refer to as "our universe"—a vast
sphere extending nearly fourteen billion light–years in all directions, or
some twenty–eight billion light–years in diameter—is only one of a
multitude of other such bubble universes stretching throughout infinity! Thinking of the foam that washes up with the waves at the seashore,
Sir Arthur Clarke has described it this way: "Many and strange are the
universes that drift like bubbles in the foam upon the River of Time."
That branch of astronomy which deals with such mind–boggling concepts is known as "cosmology." While Edgar Cayce didn't use the word
as such in the text of any of his readings, he definitely was psychically
tapping into its domain in speaking of multiple universes long before
science itself did!
    There are other striking examples of Edgar Cayce's ability to tap into
secrets of the cosmos that were not known (or at least not openly discussed) in his time yet which have become an exciting part of mainstream science today. But before exploring them, it needs to be pointed
out here that the ultra–large (the cosmos) and the ultra–small (the subatomic world) are intimately linked. Nuclear reactions between differ-

ent types of atoms, for example, cause the stars to shine. And events in the tiny invisible "quantum world" of the atom directly impact the colossal expansion of the vast universe itself—as well as the creation of matter apparently from out of nowhere! As many famous physicists, astronomers, and cosmologists have remarked, we are definitely living in an utterly amazing "Alice in Wonderland" universe.

Alternate Realities and Dimensions

Another example of Cayce's cosmic visions concerns other realities or dimensions than the one we recognize. While "realities" and "other realities" together appear in his readings more than eighty times, nearly all of these references relate to its familiar conscious and subconscious aspects rather than to cosmic ones. But there are a few in the Cayce material that do, as seen in this report from reading 254-63: "Exactly what the language mechanism was has never been explained by the readings themselves, except for very fragmentary remarks to the effect that higher–dimensional realities can not easily be expressed in three-dimensional terms." (This report was written by Dr. Gina Cerminara and appears in its entirety in Appendix 2.)

When we search under the term "other dimensions," it's another story. Appearing nearly 200 times in the text of the Cayce readings, many of them *do* have cosmic significance.

Here are just a few of the many readings in which Edgar Cayce himself spoke about other dimensions:

> Yet the entity has experiences in the fourth, the fifth, yea to the seventh dimensions.   2850-1

> For, the earth-consciousness rarely conceives of that which may not be of a three-dimensional nature. The fourth and fifth dimensions may be spoken of, but as to their proofs— to most, and even to this entity at times—these are hazy.
>   2771-1

So, in attempting to give an entity such as this the information as to its experiences through material sojourns, the urges that arise from the application of lessons attained in other dimensions, it is like attempting to describe that for which we have little or no vocabulary—in that particular realm of thought or activity.   2559-1

Yet as the mental and the spiritual become more and more expressive, or controlling through the experiences in the earth, the entity becomes aware of other dimensions in its material sojourn.   533-1

For, to be sure, each soul manifests in other dimensions through sojourns in the environs about the earth. 2462-2

The souls that are aware of their being in a consciousness as they pass through the environ, or the dimension of that consciousness. Just as in the earth it is known as three dimensions, yet man may think in an eight-dimensional consciousness.   3037-1

Yes, we have those records which are a portion of the experience of this entity in the material plane, as well as through those dimensions in which the entity has had consciousness during the interims.   5201-1

As to the urges latent and exhibited—we find these as the combination of those efforts, those urges arising from a composite of the earthly or material experiences and the application in other dimensions, or through the periods of transition in the earth.   3674-1

Remember, there are material urges and there are materials in other consciousnesses not three-dimensions alone.
                                     5366-1

As we find, then, these are latent and manifested urges from consciousness in realms which may be termed astrological aspects and yet this is not the true word or the meaning of same. For it is the consciousness of the entity in other phases or dimensions that cannot be expressed in words of three-dimensional meanings, and thus we give them general terms or names . . .   5102-1

Urges latent and manifested arise from sources within the experience of the entity. All of former appearances or activities of the soul-entity in other spheres or dimensions have left their imprint.   2610-1

(Q) Is there but one spirit force manifesting in various dimensions, yet all one force, separating into portions by virtue subsidiary force? That is, of mind and consciousness?
(A) All one force. One spirit force, one harmonious force, each varying in the degree of their ability to manifest the whole.   900-89

As to urges arising from sojourns in the earth, and the indwelling through the periods of activity in other dimensions, we find latent and manifested forces according to that the entity cultivates within itself.   2612-1

In giving the interpretations of the records here, there are a great deal of activities of the entity in the earth plane, as well as urges latent from the consciousnesses in those realms of other dimensions than the earth.   5082-1

The interims between earthly expressions are indicated. To the entity here, the expression has been in those environs or consciousnesses or dimensions, through those periods; yet remaining within the same active force or the

universe—or the earth and the sun, the moon and the
planets about the earth.   3333-1

Astrological aspects—not because the stars were in such a
position, but because of the activities of the entity as an
entity through that consciousness accredited to the various phases or dimensions of activity—we find in the earth
plane the three dimensions, in Venus the four, in Jupiter
the five, in Uranus the seven—all of these; not as of planes,
as sometimes spoken of, but consciousnesses—the ability
to reason from certain activities.   3006-1

Not that the entity lives as an earthly being in those
environs but that the consciousness passed through the
awareness in those dimensions. For, as has been indicated,
as the earth is three-dimensional, so are other dimensions
indicated in other realms of consciousness.   4053-1

If there is drawn an analysis from the material sojourns
and the realms of consciousnesses in the various dimensions between the material sojourns, these we find somewhat as the characteristics in the personality and individu-
ality of the entity.   5070-1

Note that in many of these readings, other dimensions are discussed
in terms of being in realms of consciousness rather than in materiality.
This is most fascinating, for today many theoretical physicists, astronomers, and cosmologists not only believe that our thoughts create our
own reality—but that they literally create the universe we perceive as
well (a concept that will be explored further). This includes all of its
various physical properties and multiple dimensions, ranging in size
from the subatomic world to the very galaxies themselves!

Superstring Theory

This leads us into another related and equally profound aspect of Edgar Cayce's readings regarding the cosmos. Keeping in mind what was said earlier in this chapter about the link between the ultra-small and ultra-large, we examine next one of the hottest topics in physics and cosmology today—that of "string theory." Also known as "superstring theory," it posits that all matter is made of tiny invisible strands of vibrating energy, differing frequencies of vibration accounting for the multitude of elementary particles making up the atom and in turn the physical world itself. Many believe that this may be the long-sought-after Holy Grail of physics, known variously as the "grand unification theory," the "theory of everything," and the "unified field theory." It seeks to describe all the forces of nature as actually being the result of just a single comprehensive force.

The mathematics of this exciting concept requires a multidimensional model of reality—one having at least eleven dimensions for its existence. And here we find some amazing similarities between superstring theory and the discussions of vibration and multiple dimensions found in the Cayce material. Vibration itself is such a key concept that "vibration" appears over 1,300 times and "vibratory forces" well over 600 times in various contexts (mostly medical) within the text of the readings! (Mention must be made here of a wonderful reference by the A.R.E. Press entitled *Edgar Cayce on Vibrations: Spirit in Motion*, written by the A.R.E.'s executive director, Kevin Todeschi.) The following is a sampling of some of the fascinating information about vibration and other dimensions found in the readings:

> Then to the entity we would counsel thus: Learn the lesson of the interpreting of the dimensions of the earth, or that the three-dimensions in the mind may be seven, and in spirit eleven and twelve and twenty-two.   5149-1

> That inter-between, that which is, that of which, that from one object to another when in matter is of the same nature, or what that is what the other is, only changed in its

vibration to produce that element, or that force, as is termed in man's terminology as *dimensions* of space, or *dimensions* that give it, whatever may be the solid, liquid, gas, or what *its form* or dimension!   364-6

To begin with this, as to be understandable, we must first consider that which is and that which we know of as a given law. We know that all force is created by vibration. We know that all vibration becomes electrical in its action and its effect. That is, it enlivens, bring[s] greater vibration, or being under vibration becomes deadened or destructive to one or the other of the vibrations thus met.

That law governing then the vibrations in transmission of messages, as is called radio, is the relativity of vibration as set in motion in any one particular place, and other vibrations attuned to that same vibration receiving through the electrical waves, created by the one through the receiving forces, magnified in the other . . .

All force (for the law again) we find is ever present in every atom of vibration, and is subject to all laws of heat and cold and of the other vibrations in the air, or in the vacuum created from time to time by changes, this creating more effect on the vibratory force than other vibrations, for each are in themselves.   2492-5

Before that the entity was in the Lemurian land, as one interpreting the laws of gravity, the laws of electrical vibration as might be applied to the usefulness of material beings.   2850-1

For it is not strange that music, color, vibration are all a part of the planets, just as the planets are a part—and a pattern—of the whole universe.   5755-1

Then, as applying same, the entity finds that the whole

lesson, then, is that as has been given. All matter is as one matter. All time as one time, and the various conditions as are presented in that of the material plane, is as to the rate of its vibratory force as is set in motion, and its portion of that first Creative Energy that impels its own propagation, in time, in space, in the material form and manner, and is of man's—the highest created Creative Energy in the material plane—the set spaces by man.   900-306

First, let it be understood there is the pattern in the material or physical plane of every condition as exists in the cosmic or spiritual plane, for things spiritual and things material are but those same conditions raised to a different condition of the same element—for all force is as of one force   5756-4

Provocative Insights

In addition to the above readings, the following fascinating commentary about vibration, strings, and other dimensions appears in the Cayce material as a report written by one of Edgar Cayce's major supporters, Morton Blumenthal. He was intimately familiar with Cayce's work, and had discussed such concepts with him not only in readings for himself but also in person.

"We also know that things that occupy space, as well as space itself, are but forms of motions, as science has indicated. But motion or vibration is what our sensations and ideas tell us it is, just as are the crystalized forms of motions, namely, space and things that occupy space are what our sensations and ideas tell us they are. Therefore, the limitation of our mind limits our knowledge of what motion or vibration is, just as it limits our knowledge of that which vibration acts to become in crystalized form of material things (chairs, tables, houses, trees, animals, etc.), and the space these things occupy. Motion or vibration is a phenomenon, or result of some, to our limited finite minds; an unknowable infinite quality that composes the substance of space, and all things that occupy space, including our own selves.

This substance that is doing the moving or vibrating is unknowable to our sensations and to our three-dimensional physical mind, because this infinite substance of infinite space is not measurable in terms of finite three dimensions. We know one house, is different from another house because both houses are separated from each other by space, or in other words, one house and the other house, and the space that divides the two houses are different independent three-dimensional realities, because our physical minds so operate as to make the world, (whatever it may be in reality), become for us divided into different three-dimensional realities. Yet science, (and I refer you to Dr. Whitney's experiments), has reduced the two houses and space to one and the same primal element, namely, to the essence of motion or vibration, whatever that primal element may be. We do not know what this primal element is, because it is not measurable in terms of three dimensions, and our physical mind so operates as to only be able to measure in limited, finite terms of three dimensions, namely, length, height and breadth. Our mind separates things into those classifications, bounded by the three dimensions of height, breadth and depth. Thus one three-dimensional object called house, is made by the operation of our physical or objective mind to be separated from another limited three-dimensional, physical reality, called house, by a third three-dimensional physical property called space. But science has reduced space and things that occupy space to one source, namely, motion or vibration. It says houses and space are but *forms* of vibration. The substance that is doing the vibrating in materialized form is the same as that which is vibrating to become celestial forms, or bodies (stars, planets, etc.) says Dr. Whitney. Thus, in substance, this essence is not to be divided off into different three-dimensional sections, but is one in essence whether in that *form* called space, or that form called things, and which latter we say, occupy or exist in space."   (1800-15 Reports)

A Mind-Expanding Experience

We'll explore Edgar Cayce's visionary concepts about the universe and the role of vibration further in the chapter on gravity and cosmology. But those readers desiring to learn more about multiple dimensions and superstring theory should consult the provocative book *The Elegant Universe: Superstrings, Hidden Dimensions and the Quest for the Ultimate Theory* by Brian Greene (W.W. Norton and Company, 2003). Better yet, watch the superb three-hour *Nova* television special of the same name based on the book itself, available from PBS at their Web site (PBS.org). Interviews with noted physicists, astronomers, and cosmologists are combined with state-of-the-art visuals and special effects to create what can only be described as an utterly mind-expanding (some would say mind-blowing) experience!

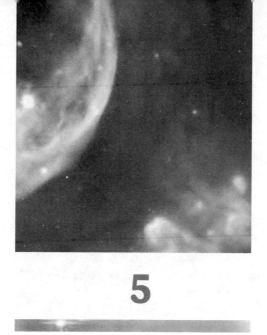

5

Astronomy and Astrology

THE GREAT RIFT

I well remember speaking on behalf of astronomy at a major annual astrology conference a few years ago. One well-known astrologer spent a full hour discussing the influence of the planet Jupiter on our lives. When he finished, a lady in the audience politely asked him, "Well, just where is Jupiter in the sky tonight?" He immediately barked back at her, "Don't ask me—ask him [referring to myself]. He's the astronomer!" This event is so telling, for he obviously was going strictly by his complex astrological "charts" but knew nothing about where the planet was actually located in the sky that night or on any other one. (Incidentally, Jupiter *was* shining brightly over our heads as we all left the auditorium at the end of the program!)

The great rift and resulting controversy between astronomy and astrology (actually astronomers and astrologers!) has raged for as long as one can remember. The former totally dismisses the latter as sheer folly and charlatanism (despite the fact that Johannes Kepler—one of the most famous astronomers in history—was also an astrologer), while the latter totally ignores even the most basic astronomical facts. Another concern is the complete disregard by most astrologers for such exciting and cosmically significant objects as black holes, neutron stars, pulsars, magnetars, and quasars—all of which have gravitational and other influences on our planet and ourselves. You've probably met many Aquarians but I'll bet you've never met an Ophiuchian. But you should have if astrology is fully valid, for there is actually a thirteenth "sign" of the zodiac. It's the huge constellation Ophiuchus, the Serpent Bearer, sitting astride the ecliptic between Scorpius and Sagittarius, as any star chart will show. And like you, I've never met an Ophiuchian!

Some idea of the disdain astronomers have for astrology can be gleaned from the following fact. The Astronomical Society of the Pacific—one of this country's largest associations of professional (and many amateur) astronomers—offers on its web site an "Astrology Defense Kit" designed to help combat the "vermin" of this popular "pseudoscience." Included are "Ten Embarrassing Questions" to ask an astrologer. This, in turn, originally appeared in the August 1988 issue of *Sky & Telescope* magazine, the world's leading astronomical publication. You can view the defense kit at: http://www.astrosociety.org/education/astro/act3/astrology3.html.

An Historic Conference

In an historic attempt to help heal the rift between these two subjects, Steven Forrest—one of the world's best-known and respected astrologers, having formal training in both physics and astronomy—and I convinced the A.R.E. to sponsor a conference in Virginia Beach on "Reviving the Natural Unity of Astrology and Astronomy" in March 2004. Also participating as a speaker was Raye Mathis, another gifted astrologer known to many A.R.E. members. Numerous astrologers and those interested in astrology from all across the country and abroad attended. However, I was the *only* astronomer willing to speak at or attend this landmark conference; such is the indifference of the astronomical community!

As a prelude to this gathering, an article entitled "What Lies Ahead? An Astrological Forecast for 2004" was published by Raye Mathis in the January/February 2004 issue of the A.R.E.'s membership magazine, *Venture Inward*. It's well worth reading if you have access to back issues of this excellent publication. A truly superb reference combining astronomy, physics, and cosmology with astrology is Steven Forrest's classic work *The Night Speaks* (ACS Publications, 2003). Though the book is currently out-of-print, the author plans to reissue it; find information on this and his other publications at SevenPawsPress.com.

Cayce's Disclaimer

A huge number of Edgar Cayce's readings have to do with various astrological aspects of a person's past and present lives (especially their astrological sojourns). And so how do we justify this in view of what has already been said above? To begin with, Cayce repeatedly stated in reading after reading that the stars and planets and other celestial bodies *do not* control or determine our lives! Below is a sampling of his remarks to that effect (the emphases being Cayce's):

> ... *but let it be understood here, no action of any planet or the phases of the sun, the moon or any of the heavenly bodies surpass the rule of man's will power, the* power given by the Creator of man, in the beginning, when he became a living soul, with the power of choosing for himself.   3744-4

> It is not then because an entity was born at a certain season, or a certain phase of the moon, or a certain period of the sun's position to the earth, or any of the planets, or the position of this or that phase of the outer consciousness. But it is because of the entity's application of *self in respect to what* these planets or constellations bring by association of its activities. And thus the relative relationships may become a part of the awareness of the entity. 1776-1

Astrological urges are not existent because of the position of the sun, moon or any planet at the time of birth, but rather because the soul-entity is a part of the Universal Consciousness and has dwelt in those environs. Thus they yield, or wield, an influence upon individual application of spiritual and mental truths or laws, *as* they are brought into material manifestations.   2132-1

As to the influences from the various zodiacal signs— these are not because the sun or the moon or any of the planets are in a certain position, but because of the soul's activity there, and what the entity has done about *truth* as truth!   3084-1

And the other stars, the sun, the moon were all given to be the servants and not rulers of man. Don't forget it!
                                                        3356-1

As for astrological aspects—the entity's experience in the present has been and would be almost contradictory to any of those aspects accorded to the activities of the entity because of the position of this or that planet or star, or this or that phase of the astrological aspects. [!]   2185-1

Astronomy and Astrology

Perhaps the best discourse by Edgar Cayce on the relationship be-tween astronomy and astrology is found within the following reading:

When the heavens and the earth came into being, this meant the universe as the inhabitants of the earth know same; yet there are many suns in the universe—those even about which our sun, our earth, revolve; and all are mov-ing toward some place—yet space and time appear to be incomplete.

Then time and space are but one. Yet the sun, that is the center of this particular solar system, is the center; and, as has been indicated and known of old, it is that about which the earth and its companion planets circulate, or evolve [revolve? (Question is by stenographer of reading)]

The beginnings of the understanding of these, and their influences upon the lives of individuals, were either thought out, evolved or interpreted by those of old, without the means of observing same as considered today necessary in order to understand.

Astronomy is considered a science and astrology as foolishness. Who is correct? One holds that because of the position of the earth, the sun, the planets, they are balanced one with another in some manner, some form; yet that they have nothing to do with man's life or the expanse of life, or the emotions of the physical being in the earth.

Then, why and how do the effects of the sun *so* influence other life in the earth and not affect *man's* life, man's emotions?

As the sun has been set as the ruler of this solar system, does it not appear to be reasonable that it *has* an effect upon the inhabitants of the earth, as well as upon plant and mineral life in the earth?

Then if not, why, how did the ancients worship the sun *as* the representative of a continuous benevolent and beneficent influence upon the life of the individual?

Thus as we find given, the sun and the moon and the stars were made also—this being the attempt of the writer to convey to the individual the realization that there *is* an influence in their activity! For, remember, they—the sun, the moon, the planets—have their marching orders from the divine, and they move in same.   5757-1

Astrological Influences

Having now established these important perspectives, let's next see what the readings actually *do* have to say about astrological influences (in addition to reinforcing all of the foregoing). We're instructed in one reading:

> (Q) Would it be well for me to make a study of astrology?
> (A) Well for everyone to make a study of astrology! for, as indicated, while many individuals have set about to prove the astrological aspects and astrological survey enable one to determine future as well as the past conditions, these are well to the point where the individual understands that these act upon individuals because of their sojourn or correlation of their associations with the environs through which these are shown—see? Rather than the star directing the life, the life of the individual directs the courses of the stars, see? . . . It may be said that the line of thought in the present is towards a change in the Aries age from the Pisces, or from the Aquarius, or to those various activities, see? But it doesn't mean that every individual changes, for each individual has its own development. As we look about us we see the various spheroïds, spheres, planets or solar systems, and they have their individual activity. Look at the soul of man and know it may be equal to, or greater; for it must be man's ability to control one of such! Vast study, yes!   311-10

Likewise, we're told in another reading:

> (Q) Every astrologer erecting a chart for . . .
> (A) (Interrupting) We have little or nothing to contribute to the interest self evinces in astrology. Not that there are not definite helps to be attained from astrology, but those who live by same the more oft are controlled rather than controlling their own lives and their destinies. Astrology is

a fact, in most instances. But astrological aspects are but
signs, symbols. *No influence* is of greater value or of greater
help than the *will* of an individual. Use such directions as
stepping stones. Do not let them become stumbling stones
in thy experience.   815-6

And while sojourns themselves are the subject of another chapter,
the following readings hopefully will help clarify just what the actual
astrological influences are:

In giving that which would be helpful from the interpretations of the records here, it would be well for the entity to
bear in mind that the sojourns in the environs about the
earth have as much to do with the place and time of birth
as the position of a planet, star or element has upon the
entity in the earth's plane—or more. Sojourns in environments are those innate activities, while sojourns in the
earth are those of the emotional natures; yet each one is
under the influence more of the will—or what an entity
does about an urge—than merely the position of a sojourn
of the entity. Although there are influences from the
astrological angle, they are as signs, omens and impulses;
not as destinies, for the destiny of each soul is in what the
entity does about the application of creative influences
and forces in its own experience in any environ.   820-1

That those influences from astrological aspects are arising
as urges is true. Not because of the position of a star or
planet, or any sign of the zodiac, but rather because of what
one has done about what each of those planets or environs
represents in the existence, in the consciousness of the
individual entity, as related *to* the whole of the Creative
Force in the entity's experience.   1562-1

If a composite were made of the urges arising from the

sojourns during the interims between material appearances, or the astrological aspects, we find certain inclinations. For these, the astrological aspects represent the
interims between the material or earthly awarenesses. For
the soul, to be sure, is aware and active in other
consciousnesses than the three-dimensional. For as the
soul is in this particular solar system, it is subject to—and
active in—all those phases of awareness in same. Some call
it astrology, some call it foolishness; yet, as indicated, these
influences do not supplant the will.   3062-2

In analyzing urges there are those that are latent and
manifested not only from the sojourns in the earth, but
from the manner in which the entity, the self, has applied
the lessons ye have gained from period to period in other
realms. These are spoken of as astrological, but not as
ordinary terms of astrology, but rather as an awareness in
the dimensions. Thus, ye know the God-head in three
dimensions. Thus ye know self in three dimensions; but in
Jupiter, in Venus, in Saturn, ye know other dimensions
than those in body-physical. Ye experience same, but as in
a consciousness, comparable to that realm itself.   5177-1

Hence there *are* urges, or influences—not as astrological
aspects but from sojourns through which the entity has
passed—or experiences during the interims between
earthly manifestations. These become manifested in the
dreams, the hopes; while the earthly sojourns find expression in the emotions of the body; and not because a star, a
constellation, or even any phase of the zodiac sign, was in
such and such a position at the time of birth.   2549-1

In interpreting the urges latent and manifested as we find
them here—there are urges arising from astrological aspects—or the sojourns during the interims between earthly

incarnations. These are not always easy to interpret into material words, yet these may be indicated for this particular entity. The astrological urges are not existent merely because of the position of the planets, or any phase of so called astrology, but because of a consciousness in an environ interpreted in the name of planets—that are as companions with the earth in its journey through this particular phase of the universe, or universal consciousness.

Here, for this entity, we find Venus, Mercury, Jupiter, Saturn and Uranus as the names, or environs, or consciousnesses, in which activities are indicated.

2437-1

Note in this last reading that Cayce actually indicated (as he nearly always did) just what planetary environs the entity (the person for whom the reading was being given) had visited between earthly reincarnations. Dealing solely with the physical characteristics of these other worlds as astronomy and space science do is apparently looking at only one aspect of their significance in the grand cosmic scheme of things. It's also essential to look at them through the spiritual eyes of the soul to grasp their full wonder and import.

Psychic Anchors?

Ending here on a personal note, as an astronomer I still do have my doubts about many of the tenets of astrology as it's practiced today. But I'm also open-minded enough to recognize that there are some important truths to be found within it—as clearly demonstrated by both the Cayce readings themselves and the no-nonsense approach to the subject by my esteemed colleague, astrologer/astronomer/physicist Steven Forrest, mentioned earlier. My personal suspicion is that maybe planets, stars, constellations, and other celestial objects act as "psychic anchors" in much the same way as do tarot cards, crystal balls, and palms for gifted psychic readers in general. And perhaps support for this view in the Cayce material is to be found in the following:

> The entity then was a sand reader, or one who interpreted
> the sands in the capacity of what might be called a sooth-
> sayer, or a crystal gazer, or a star addict.   3356-1

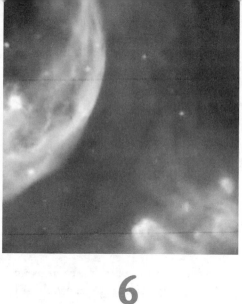

6

Planetary/Astrological/Astral Sojourns Within Our Solar System

SOJOURNS DEFINED

As a verb, the word "sojourn" is defined by *Webster's Dictionary* as meaning "to live somewhere temporarily, as on a visit; stay for a while" and, likewise as a noun, as "a brief or temporary stay; visit." The Cayce readings are full of references to the sojourns of many individuals (including Edgar himself!) for whom he was asked to explore their past lives. These are variously described as "astrological," "planetary," and "astral" in nature—and nearly all of them relate to visits to the various planets of our solar system. They can also be viewed as "soul journeys," since it is the soul that actually does the traveling to these other realms in the spiritual rather than in the physical body. The following readings are a just a few of the many that make this clear:

> Seek then, ye, in understanding as to where, why, from
> what source, there may be gained the experiences of an

entity, a soul, through its journeys in this the odic sphere, or through that known as this solar system. Each portion of that one whole, in that we call life, as it uses the attributes of the physical forces of a created form manifested in a material world, makes a record; as truly as is seen in the cylinder of the plate of the phonograph, or as is given to the radio transmitter upon the ethers of a material world.

254-68

As to the astrological aspects, then, or those phases of experience of this entity outside the earth, those phases of consciousness are known by those influences that are accredited to and are a portion of the mental and soul experience in those planets that make up the realm of the earthly environ.

That is, as the Sun is the source of life in materiality in the earth, the beauty of the satellite of the earth in the Moon in dwellings from which individual or soul experiences (not personally) travel in the planets within this same realm, *all* are a portion of the entity's experience or soul experience in its passage.   805-4

As has so oft been given, an individual experience in the earth plane is motivated by that which arises from its sojourns in the influences of the consciousnesses outside of the physical being—or as ye would say astrologically the sojourn in the environ of Venus, Jupiter, Mars, Neptune, Saturn, Uranus, Sun, Moon, and the constellations and those effects upon same—emotionally from the *innate* forces; *and* by the *emotional* effect from sojourns in the earth. Both of these are witnesses.   281-33

While the spheres of this particular solar system are given names, do not interpret same as the entity living in the same physical consciousness on Venus, Jupiter, Mercury

or Uranus, as experienced in a three-dimensional plane.
2753-2

Having stated that sojourns are not in the physical body, the author, however, has always looked upon two readings with fascination that may indicate that—just perhaps—there actually *is* some form of physicality involved in at least a few of these travels. (More will be said about this in the discussion of astral sojourns below.) Those two readings are:

As it has been often presented by one school of thought, the dwellers upon the Moon (the satellite of the earth) preceded the abilities for matter (expressed in a form that is known as matter in the earth). And this entity was among those that so dwelt, and is influenced by two sojourns there.   264-31

For, much might be given respecting those environs and as to how or why there have been and are accredited to the various planets certain characterizations that make for the attractions of souls' sojourns in that environ. But these are places of abode. As in the earth we find the elements are peopled, as the earth has its own moon or satellites enjoined in its environ, so is it with the other planets. The earth with its three-fourths water, with its elements, is peopled; yes. So are the various activities in other solar systems.   541-1

Worlds Visited and Not Visited

Following is a listing of those bodies in our solar system to which people for whom Edgar Cayce gave readings had traveled in their sojourns. While it is the astrological influences that are discussed in so many of these readings rather than physical ones, it still may be of interest to briefly summarize some of the physical characteristics of these worlds (especially in view of what was discussed in the previous section). Following each object's official and popular name is its average distance from the Sun, its diameter, revolution period about the Sun (its "year"), rotation period (its "day"), temperature, atmosphere if any, and number of moons known as of the time of writing. Can you visualize yourself as being present physically on these different worlds? Does anything about them seem "familiar" to you? If so, you may have actually been there in a past incarnation (in one form or another)!

Sun: Our Daytime Star; distance (from us) 93,000,000 miles; diameter 864,000 miles; rotation period 25 days at equator; temperature at visible "surface" 10,000 degrees F/20,000,000 degrees F in its thermonuclear core; atmosphere/composition mainly hydrogen.

Moon: Luna/Earth's Satellite; distance (from us) 239,000 miles; diameter 2160 miles; revolution period (about Earth) 28 days; rotation period 28 days; temperature +215 to − 240 degrees F; no detectable atmosphere.

Mercury: The Elusive One; distance 36,000,000 miles; diameter 3,000 miles; revolution period 88 days; rotation period 59 days; temperature +440 to −280 degrees F; trace atmosphere; no moons.

Venus: The Morning/Evening Star/Earth's Sister Planet; distance 67,000,000 miles; diameter 7520 miles; revolution period 225 days; rotation period 243 days; temperature +890 degrees F; super−dense carbon dioxide and sulfuric acid atmosphere; no moons.

Mars: The Red Planet (actually orange!); distance 142,000,000 miles; diameter 4,200 miles; revolution period 687 days; rotation period 24.6 hours; temperature −120 to −20 degrees F; thin carbon dioxide atmosphere; 2 moons.

Jupiter: The Giant Planet; distance 484,000,000 miles; diameter 88,850 miles; revolution period 12 years; rotation period 10 hours; temperature −220 degrees F; dense hydrogen and helium atmosphere; 63 moons.

Saturn: The Ringed Planet; 886,000,000 miles; diameter (planet) 74,900 miles/(rings) 165,000 miles; revolution period 29.5 years; rotation period 10.5 hours; temperature −290 degrees; dense hydrogen and helium atmosphere; 56 moons.

Uranus: The Green Planet; distance 1,800,000,000 miles; diameter 31,765 miles; revolution period 84 years; rotation period 17 hours; temperature −300 degrees F; hydrogen and methane atmosphere; 27 moons.

Neptune: The Blue Planet; distance 2,800,000,000 miles; diameter 30,775 miles; revolution period 165 years; rotation period 16 hours; temperature −325 degrees F; hydrogen and methane atmosphere; 13 moons.

Pluto: Kuiper Belt World; distance 3,700,000,000 miles; diameter 1,430 miles; revolution period 248 years; rotation period 6.4 days; temperature −350 degrees F; possible trace atmosphere; 3 moons.

Interestingly, no mention was made in the readings of sojourns to the satellites of the planets (other than our own Moon). This is rather surprising since several of the moons of the giant planets are bigger than Mercury and have fascinating physical characteristics uniquely their own—as, for example, a number harboring ice-covered liquid water oceans and organic compounds! Also, the larger asteroids like 600-mile-diameter Ceres and great comets such as Halley's or Hale-Bopp having sizeable nuclei were not cited. Perhaps the reason lies in the fact that these neglected bodies have been assigned no role in classical astrology. The same surely goes for Eris—the 1,500-mile-diameter ice-ball planet lying beyond Pluto, some 6,400,000,000 miles from the Sun—which wasn't even discovered until 2005.

Of the hundreds of times the Moon is mentioned by Edgar Cayce, actual sojourns there (as opposed to its purely astrological influences) appear to be specifically cited in only one case—that found in 264-31 given above. So what about our radiant Daytime Star? The Sun appears more than 600 times in the text of the Cayce readings alone. However, most of these references concern its medical aspects and astrological influences, the following being just two typical examples of the latter:

> The sun is a great influence in the experience of the entity.
> 1724-4

> Astrologically, then—we find Venus, Mercury and Jupi-
> ter, with the Sun and the other constellations coming as
> influences.   2988-2

Just as in the case of the Moon, actual sojourns to the Sun were
rarely mentioned as such by Cayce. Here are a couple of instances where
they were at least implied by him:

> This door once opened and realized in thy heart, in thy
> mind, in thy soul, no one may surpass thee in thy accom-
> plishments. For they are many, as indicated not only in the
> astrological or solar sojourns but in thy material experi-
> ences in the earth.   3376-2

> As to the astrological aspects—these, as we judge them, are
> rather from the realms of activity of the entity during those
> interims between the material or earthly sojourns; and
> come in Venus, the sun, Jupiter, Uranus, Saturn. 1837-1

There are two interesting asides worth mentioning here. Up until
about 200 years ago many astronomers (including Sir William Herschel,
discoverer of the planet Uranus and the "Father of Observational Astronomy") believed that *all* the bodies of the solar system were inhabited—including the Sun itself! While their belief is scoffed at by
astronomers today, in the context of the sojourns and soul travels mentioned by Edgar Cayce, they were certainly right! And we hear much in
astrology about the influences of the various heavenly bodies on us,
but here's one in the Cayce readings about *our influence on them*—in this
case involving none less than the Sun itself:

> Then, what are the sun spots? A natural consequence of
> that turmoil which the sons of God in the earth reflect
> upon same.   5757-1

How utterly amazing and profoundly significant!

And now to the sojourn readings themselves. Note here that the astrological influences of the Sun, Moon, and various planets are so well-
known and covered in so many existing books on astrology that they
are not being repeated here. (One excellent reference is *Edgar Cayce's
Astrology for the Soul* by Margaret Gammon and W.H. Church, available
from the A.R.E. Press.) The emphasis instead is on what Edgar Cayce had
to say about the effect of sojourns to these other worlds had in general
(the first reading below being a very informative discourse on this), as
well as specific impacts of these visits, on the person for whom the
reading was given.

Astrological Sojourns

> Hence the awareness of the soul as to its separateness, or its
> being separated, only comes through the manifestations
> of the principles of that cosmic consciousness in material-
> ity. Hence it is as evolution in a part of the development of
> the whole of the universe; not this consciousness of our
> own solar system, but of that about all solar force, or which
> our own system is only a mere part of the whole conscious-
> ness. But in the earth and man's awareness into the three-
> dimensional consciousness, only those that have entered
> same may relieve [re-leave?] or leave same through the
> awareness of there being those influences through their
> various spheres of activity, including not only the earthly
> sojourns or material sojourns as we know in a physical
> consciousness, but the sojourns throughout the spheres of
> activity when they are absent from a physical or material
> consciousness.   1602-3

The earthly sojourns make for rather the innate and manifested urges that come from the emotional forces of the
body, while the astrological sojourns make for rather the
mental urges.   189-3

In giving that which may be helpful to the entity in the
present, the approach to the astrological influences would
be from the sojourns rather than the position of the planets or the elements in same. For, the sojourns make for
innate influences; while the earth's appearances make for
the greater urge within the present mental forces of the
entity.   444-1

In entering the present experience, we find that astrological sojourns as well as environmental influences in earth's
indwelling have their innate or direct influence upon the
mental and material forces of the present entity.   380-1

In the light of what has been the experience of the entity,
it is well that the question be asked and understood: How
or why in this particular experience would that of a numerological nature be more influencing or influential in
the psychic experiences of the entity than the urges from
astrological sojourns in the various spheres of activity or
development?   338-3

As we find, those that may be the more helpful, applicable
and practical in the present experience, would be—we
would direct—from the astrological sojourns, rather than
from other inclinations; for these, as we find, deal more
directly with the mental and material inclinations of an
entity in most appearances in the earth.   373-2

Then we have the influences from the astrological sojourns, the material sojourns and what the entity in the

various realms did about the opportunities offered in those consciousnesses.   2402-2

In giving the interpretations—these we find may be given as a composite of the effects, or the urges in the entity's experience from material as well as the astrological sojourns.   2000-3

So, the astrological sojourns are rather as intuitional influences felt when in meditation or distress in mind, that brings the harking of a something that may be found through the application of self respecting the knowledge self has concerning the Creative Forces in a material world.
                                                                  439-1

In entering the present experience from the astrological aspects, we find these in the present experience would rather be confusing were they accepted from that commonly given from the astrological aspect only. Yet these with the sojourns in the earth have made and do make for influences in the experience that have been had, or that may be experienced in the present sojourn.

Those from the astrological sojourns would be that interim from the earth's appearance to the next earthly experience.   509-1

Planetary Sojourns

Know that the planetary influence or the astrological nature is as something *innate*, while the sojourns in the earth are of that known as sensuous or magnified or expressed or manifested in the *beings* of the entity through the emotions of the body.   1219-1

(Q) An entity only has a soul number when in the earth plane.

(A) Yes.

(Q) Through other planetary sojourns an entity has the opportunity to change its rate of vibration so as to be attracted in the earth plane under another soul number.

(A) Each planetary influence vibrates at a different rate of vibration. An entity entering that influence enters that vibration; not necessary that he change, but it is the grace of God that he may! It is part of the universal consciousness, the universal law.   281-55

Such influences from planetary sojourns are as urges. As to what the activities in the experience will be, or as to what the entity does about same (such urges) depends much upon the will and that the entity has made or does make as its ideal—whether mental, material *or* spiritual.   1082-3

(Q) Now, then, is it possible for an ego itself either receding through what we call interstellar space, or existing on another planet, to so keep in touch or so be aware of little finite details on the earth plane as to guide in detail regarding physical affairs, one whom that ego may choose to guide?

(A) That is correct; this is possible, but the care must be taken by such an one that they be guided in that contact from one receding through stellar space, by the same desire as is made manifest by one so receding, and seeking to aid a loved one, whether psychical character, or of the purport, intent, or friends' character, see?   136-83

(Q) Is it true that day and night are condensed or miniature copies of incarnations into the earth and into planetary or spiritual sojourns: they in turn being miniature copies of what took place in the Beginning?

(A) Very good, if you understood just what all this means! It's a very good illustration of that which has just been given; as to how there is the evolution of the soul, evolution of the mind, but not evolution of matter—save through mind, and that which builds same.   262-56

From the planetary or environmental sojourns of the entity, other than in earth, we find these run rather true to form with planetary influence; than that given in some directions from astrological data.   338-2

As we have given from the *earth's* sojourns, these vary only in the materialization, and the mentalization, and spiritualization, in the planetary sojourns.   339-1

In entering the present experience, we find those influences that may be termed purely astrological being rather secondary—even in impulses—to those from environs through earth's experiences. Not that the sojourns on the planets have not had, and do not have in the present, their influence; but these may be termed rather as moods for this entity, save at a few particular conjunctions of planetary influences when these have had more to do even then—with the material aspects (as may be termed) then mental urges.   378-12

The astrological aspects, as well as the influences from the sojourns in the earth, are only as signs, omens; producing urges, yes—latent and manifested in a different form.

Astrological influences—from planetary sojourns between the earthly interims of sojourn—are to the mental or innate self or the deeper visions or dreams, or to that which may be reached the greater through the deeper meditation.   1470-1

From the sources of the previous sojourns we find urges arising materially in the experience of the entity—that is,

from the previous earthly sojourns as well as the astrological sojourns during the interims between earthly manifestations.

Thus the earthly sojourns make for manifested urges in
the present experience. Also those planetary sojourns, in
this present solar system, make for urges that are accredited to those particular planets as states of consciousness—that become innately manifested in the present
entity.   2599-1

Astral Sojourns

For, as indicated, the urges from the astral sojourns (or
between the material activities) are upon the deeper self,
the mental; while the material sojourns produce urges
through the emotions—and thus seek expression.2031-1

In seeking entrance in the earth's plane, the entity finds the
expressions of much that has been experienced in its
sojourns under a different or varied environment. Hence
we find the astrological little in the experience of this
entity, and an ordinary version of astrological data—or of
what is ordinarily termed horoscopes—would be at vari-
ance with the experience of the entity. Not that there were
not sojourns of the entity in other environments, but
rather does the entity influence the environs in the astrological—or astral—than being ruled or governed by same.
                                                            618-3

Celestial Bodies and Astral Travel

It's obvious from the above readings that the various types of sojourns—astrological, planetary, and astral—are all just different names
for the same experience. And in connection with these journeys, here
are a few of the many fascinating Cayce readings about the astral/ethe-

real/soul/celestial/cosmic body itself (once again, all different names for the same thing) which actually does the "traveling" to other worlds:

> (Q) In regard to my first projection of myself into the astral plane, about two weeks ago: Some of the people were animated and some seemed like waxen images of themselves. What made the difference?
> (A) Some—those that appear as images—are the expressions or shells or the body of an individual that has been left when its soul self has projected on, and has not been as yet dissolved—as it were—to the realm of that activity. For what individuals are lives on and takes form in that termed by others as the astral body. The soul leaves same, and it appears as seen. Other individuals, as experienced, are in their *animated* form through their own sphere of experience at the present.   516-4

> Hence we find there are presented the same conditions in the astral or cosmic world, or cosmic consciousness, as is present in the material plane—until the consciousness of that soul has reached that development wherein such a soul is raised to that consciousness *above* the earth's sphere, or earth's attractive forces—until it reaches up, up, outward, until included in the *all*, see?   5756-4

> The body celestial or cosmic body has those attributes of the physical with the cosmic added to same, for all of hearing, seeing, understanding, becomes as *one*. Then there is that question arising, then, as to how the differentiation then in the cosmic plane. With the attempting to disseminate, divide these conditions, we find how or why the material body is unable to hear, see, gain the presence of such conditions in the cosmic, astral or celestial bodies—yet when the celestial body approaches this may come in any of the various forces as pertain to that manner

CENTER SPREAD PHOTO GALLERY

Hubble Space Telescope Sites and Images

Following are some of the most famous and stunning images from the amazing Hubble Space Telescope–our window on creation! Most of these celestial wonders have an official catalog designation (often several), which are given here for those readers who may wish to learn more about them in the literature and on the Internet. But it's their popular names that most endear them to us and make it easier to relate to them on a personal, aesthetic, and even spiritual level—wonderful names like the "Celestial Rose," the "Butterfly," and the "Fingers of God."

The author would like to address a question that's often asked about the awesomely beautiful Hubble pictures: Are the colors displayed real or have they been "doctored"? Except for certain specially enhanced images taken and/or processed for research purposes, they actually are real! This is especially true for those pictures designated "Hubble Heritage." These match exactly what the human eye would see if you were "out there" (or when you travel there in one form or another!) and were able to soak up enough photons to excite the color receptors (the cones) of your eyes.

There are something like 7,000 images now in the Hubble archives, many of the most striking of which can be viewed on your computer by going to either of the Space Telescope Science Institute's two Internet sites (hubblesite.org or stsci.edu). There you'll find not only a fantastic collection of stunning pictures to view and download , but also an amazing amount of educational information about space and the universe itself. This includes some of the latest discoveries in astronomy and cosmology made by the many scientists using the Hubble Telescope on an around–the–clock basis. All images reproduced here are courtesy of NASA, the Space Telescope Science Institute and the Hubble Heritage Team, and in a few cases the European Space Agency (ESA).

Celestial Mandalas

The primary purpose of this center spread section is to provide the reader with pictures for use in personal "open–eyed" meditation. Many find the stars and other celestial bodies ideal "celestial mandalas" for this purpose. But it should be pointed out here that you don't need the Hubble Telescope to experience this—a small backyard instrument or pair of binoculars will let you do so as well. In fact, this can be done with no optical aid at all by simply gazing at the brighter stars—especially as they are rising or setting near the horizon, at which time atmospheric turbulence causes prismatic colors to flicker and flash from their flaming hearts! And there's a very important advantage in doing so over just looking at photographs—you're actually getting photons directly in your eyes from those distant objects. This has some fantastic personal ramifications resulting from tapping into the cosmos firsthand!

In addition to their use for meditation, relaxation, and inspiration, the images presented here show us where we came from—and where we're going! As we've already seen, we are children of the stars and are literally made of stardust. Both individually and as a race, it's our cosmic destiny to ultimately return to that source! Think on this as you lose yourself in the awesome beauty and majesty of these images.

Wonders of the Solar System

Mars's Syrtis Major Region

Mars, seen on a clear day, showing its polar caps, deserts, and dark markings. The so-called Red Planet is actually orange or rust-colored—because it *is* rusty! Heating the oxidized soil would liberate both oxygen and water vapor, making it possible to terraform this planet.

A Jupiter Storm

The giant planet Jupiter spins in less than ten hours, resulting in its flattened appearance and its clouds being drawn out into parallel belts or bands. The oval at lower right is the Great Red Spot (here appearing orange in hue), which is an enormous cyclonic vortex measuring nearly 25,000 miles from tip to tip and containing organic molecules!

Ozone's Spectral Fingerprint on Ganymede

One of Jupiter's four large Galilean satellites (those discovered by Galileo) is Ganymede, seen here with a thin layer of ozone suspended above its surface. Although larger than the planet Mercury, it's one of a number of worlds in our solar system to which no one apparently has made sojourns, since none is mentioned in any of the Cayce readings.

Saturn—October 1996

The magnificent ringed planet Saturn, seen here with its rings nearly edge-on. Composed of billions of chunks of ice and rock, the rings stretch nearly 170,000 miles across—but, amazingly, are less than 100 *feet* thick in most places! While all four giant planets are now known to have systems of rings around them, none is even remotely as spectacular as Saturn's!

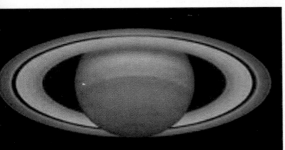

Saturn—November 2000

As Saturn orbits the Sun, its rings are tilted toward us at varying angles to our line of sight. In this picture, they are seen opened to their maximum extent. Note that there are gaps in the rings; close-up images show that there are actually *thousands* of them, making the rings appear like the grooves in some colossal cosmic phonograph record!

Neptune

Two views of the planet Neptune showing changes in its cloud tops as it rotates on its axis. This remote world looks blue due to the scattering of sunlight by its methane-rich atmosphere. In a telescope it looks icy-blue to the author—certainly appropriate for a world with temperatures hovering around 300 degrees below zero F!

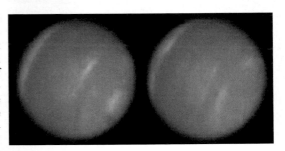

Hubble Images Comet Tempel 1 Just Before "Deep Impact" Probe Arrives

The head of Comet Tempel 1, showing its nucleus (on which NASA has landed its "Deep Impact" spacecraft!) and surrounding hazy coma. Collisions with these enormous carbon- and ice-rich "dirty snowballs," as they're referred to, are now believed to have been the major source of the water in our oceans. It's also quite likely they may have seeded them with the molecular precursors of life itself.

Wonders of Deep Space: Birth/Death of Stars

Eagle Nebula (M16) Pillar Detail Portion of Top

Here surely is a heavenly vision of pure loveliness! We are seeing a portion of the Eagle Nebula (M16) within which new stars (and their planets) are forming right before our eyes. Everything we know, including the elements of which our bodies are made, was once inside of such a stellar nursery when our own Sun and its planets first formed.

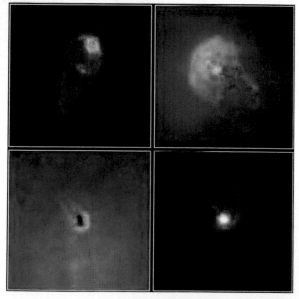

Abstract Art Found in the Orion Nebula

The Orion Nebula (M42/M43) is one of the sky's most spectacular star nurseries, only a portion of which is seen in this image. Visible to the unaided eye as a hazy "star" in Orion's sword and an interesting sight in binoculars, its magnificence in a telescope is thrilling quite beyond words!

Orion Nebula's Planetary Nurseries

Buried deep within the Orion Nebula seen above are these four amazing close-up views from Hubble showing protostars actually forming in cocoons of gas and dust. What a rare and sacred privilege to see the birth of other worlds happening right before our eyes!

Light and Shadow in the Carina Nebula (NGC 3372)

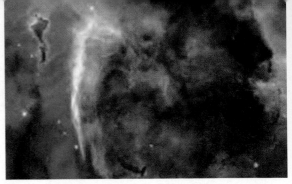

This huge molecular cloud known as the Carina Nebula (NGC 3372) reminds some of angel wings and others of a colossal cosmic beating heart.Both seem appropriate symbols for the wondrous ongoing process of birth, eventual death, and ultimate rebirth of other suns out in the depths of interstellar space.

Reflection Nebula NGC 1999

A so-called "reflection nebula" (NGC 1999), this eerie-looking object is an example of the entwined bright and dark nebulosity often found in star-forming regions. It reminds the author of a keyhole or doorway to the great cosmic beyond. Others see the silhouette of some celestial entity! What about you?

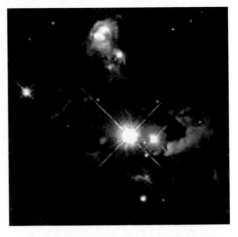

Herbig-Haro 32—Jets of Material Ejected from a Young Star

Arcs of gas and dust are seen here being ejected from a condensing new star (H-H 32) to slow its rapid spin rate—in much the same way that ice skaters slow their spin by throwing out their arms. This material, in turn, will condense to form the planets of the star.This means that worlds such as ours are a necessary byproduct of the star-birth process and, therefore, quite common in the universe.

Firestorm of Star Birth in Galaxy NGC 604

Another image illustrating the birth of stars is exceptional in that it lies in a nebula (NGC 604) *within a neighboring galaxy* more than three million light-years from us (the Triangulum or Pinwheel Galaxy/M33) rather than in our own Milky Way! Note how the knot of newborn suns surrounded by rings and shells of gas seen here closely resembles many of those found around dying stars. Star birth and star death often present similar spectacles to the awestruck onlooker.

The Ring Nebula (M57)

The Ring Nebula (M57) is one of the most beautiful examples of a planetary nebula in the entire sky, as well as one of the most famous. Material is being ejected from its central star back out into space where it originally came from. This in turn will someday form a brand-new sun! Note that the colors seen in such nebulae are a direct result of temperature, the gas glowing bluish around the hot star itself with cooler hues farther from the nucleus.

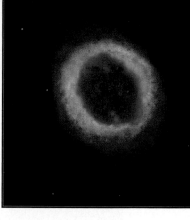

Light Echo Illuminates Dust Around Supergiant Star V838 Monocerotis

An expanding ring of debris being ejected from an elderly yellowish supergiant sun (V838 MON). This image was taken by Hubble in 2004, while the next one shows this object's appearance just two years later. While we're seeing here the latter stages in a star's life, the author prefers to look upon this wondrous scene instead as a family of young stars caressed within its nebulous womb!

Close-Up of Light Echo Around V838 Monocerotis

Photographed by Hubble in 2006—dramatic changes in the expanding nebulosity are evident in the two-year interval between pictures. With its multitinted gaseous shroud and diamondlike stars, this stunning image is an ideal one for open-eyed meditation.

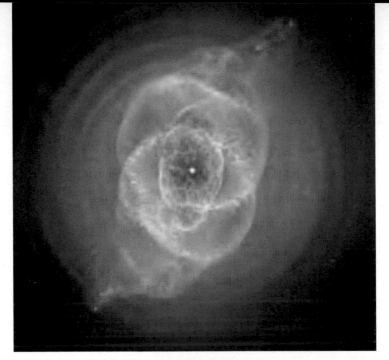

The Cat's Eye Nebula—Dying Star
Creates Fantasylike Sculpture of Gas

One of the most stunning and ethereal photographs that the Hubble Space Telescope has ever taken is that of the Cat's Eye Nebula (NGC 6543). Also known as the Snail Nebula from its appearance in large backyard telescopes, this magnificent image evokes such feelings of cosmic grandeur that it could be stared at for hours on end! It's just one example of the many such wonders that lie unsuspected over our heads on clear nights.

Scattered Light from the Boomerang Nebula

This lovely tinted example of celestial art is known as the Boomerang Nebula. Material is being ejected in two opposing directions from its dying central sun. The author personally finds stars as beautiful in their death throes as when they are being born. Perhaps there's a lesson here for the ongoing cycle of human birth and death itself?

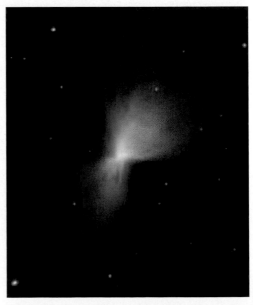

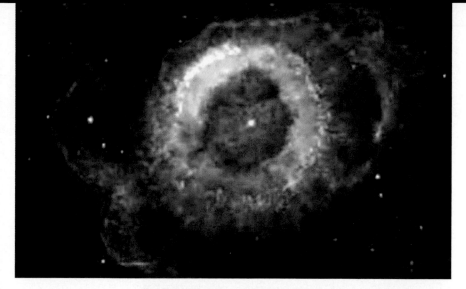

An Old Star Gives Up the Ghost

The Little Ghost Nebula (NGC 6369) offers another example of nature's colorful celestial artistry. Note especially the delicate heavenly hues, and the intricate patterns formed by the multiple rings and shells ejected by this dying star. Visually it appears quite tiny and subdued in small telescopes, leading to its unusual name.

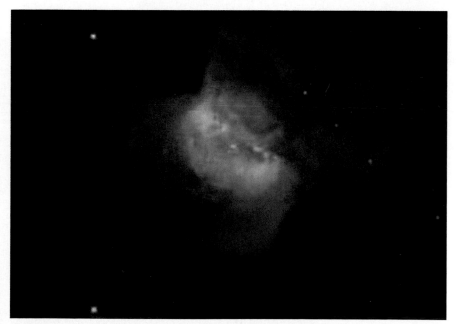

NGC 2346

Surprisingly, this lovely butterfly-wing-shaped planetary nebula (NGC 2346) has been given no popular name by stargazers despite its obvious beauty. Can you suggest one? (Note that there already is a Butterfly Nebula in the sky!) It's an example of the many bipolar planetaries in which mass is being ejected in diametrically opposed directions from the dying star as a result of intense magnetic fields surrounding it.

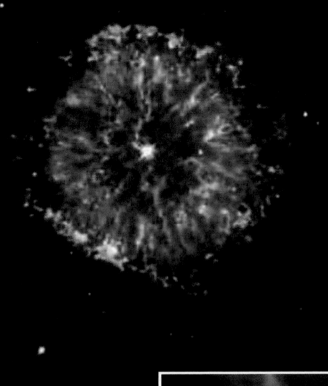

The Glowing Eye of Planetary Nebula NGC 6751

Here's a pretty nebula (NGC 6751) that bears a striking resemblance to the iris and retina of the human eye. It's an example of the symmetrical type of planetary nebulae, in contrast to the bipolar variety. Staring at it long enough gives the impression of some big celestial eye looking back at you!

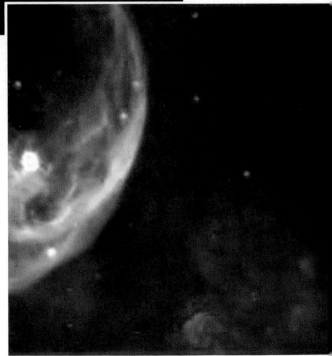

The Bubble Nebula (NGC 7635)

This beautiful image of the Bubble Nebula (NGC 7635) reminds the author of the final scene in the prophetic movie *2001: A Space Odyssey* in which the astronaut is seen enclosed within an embryonic bubble—having been reborn as a star child. The gas and dust visible in this picture are actually in the process of birth for a star itself!

The Ant Nebula (Menzel 3)—Fiery Lobes
Protrude from Dying, Sunlike Star

One of the most dramatic examples of a bipolar planetary in the sky is the appropriately named Ant Nebula (Menzel 3). Careful inspection of this image reveals multiple ejections of gas bubbles and streamers coming out of the dying star. This celestial insect is but one of an amazing variety of shapes sculptured by these aged suns on their way to the stellar graveyard.

The Spirograph Nebula (IC 418)

This striking object, known as the Spirograph Nebula (IC 418), is especially popular with those who have played with spirographs as a child. Note the countless eddies within the nebula itself and the lovely range of colors seen progressing from its hot core to its cool outer edge.

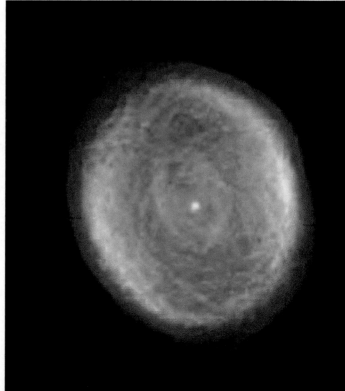

Celestial Fireworks–Sheets of Debris from a Stellar Explosion

Debris from an exploding star (N 49, DEM L 190) appears to be blowing in some celestial wind, wafting across interstellar space. In fact, that's exactly what *is* happening—the stellar "wind" being ejecta and shock waves blown out from the star itself.

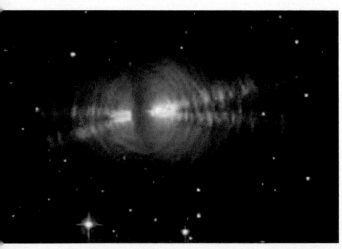

Rainbow Image of the Egg Nebula

Here's a truly unique and colorful spectacle known as the Egg Nebula (CRL 2688). Not only is this planetary nebula ejecting concentric shells of material out into space but also searchlightlike rays from its obscured nucleus. The obscuring medium itself appears to be one of those rays that's pointed directly at us. (Note that this particular image has been color enhanced for research purposes.)

Wonders of Deep Space
Stellar Systems and the Milky Way

Arches Cluster

This beautiful stellar jewelbox is known as the Arches Cluster. We are seeing only its very brightest members, for it's located close to the center of our Milky Way Galaxy—a distance of some 30,000 light-years from us. Most open star clusters lie within only a few hundred to at most a few thousand light-years of the Sun. Its stars are gravitationally bound to each other and are all moving through space together as a family.

Quintuplet Cluster

This lovely stellar commune known as the Quintuplet Cluster contains stars ranging in hue from very hot blue-white diamonds to much cooler yellow and orange gems. Seeing all these multicolored suns in the night sky from any of the planets there must be spectacular indeed!

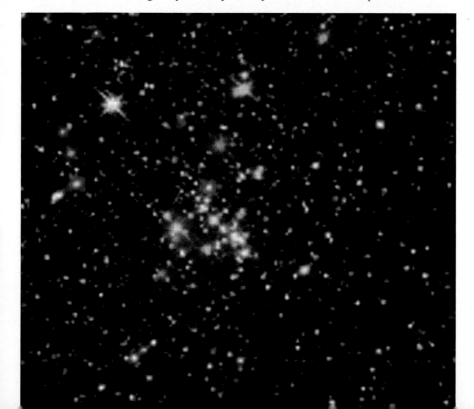

Radiant Globular Star Cluster M15

"A starry blizzard" is how some stargazers have described stellar beehives like this bright globular star cluster (M15). Containing anywhere from 50,000 up to a million suns, these swarms must contain countless numbers of life-bearing planets within them. Surprisingly there is no specific mention of sojourns to star clusters in the Cayce readings, nearly all of such travels having occurred on worlds within our own solar system. (Among the exceptions are sojourns to the bright star Arcturus—including two by Edgar Cayce himself!)

Globular Cluster M80–A Swarm of Ancient Stars in the Milky Way

Herschel's Delight (M80) is the name given to this magnificent starball by the author, because of an exalted description of it by famed observer Sir William Herschel (discoverer of the planet Uranus), as seen though his mammoth 48-inch aperture, 40-foot-long, reflecting telescope in the early 1800s. The sight of the night sky filled with countless numbers of dazzling stars from inside of globular clusters like this one must be nothing short of astounding!

Wonders of Deep Space
Galaxies and the Universe

The Small Sagittarius Star Cloud—A Sky Full of Glittering Jewels
"Stars everywhere!" best describes both this amazingly rich Hubble image—and the actual view seen through binoculars and telescopes—of the Small Sagittarius Star Cloud (M24). Others have referred to this part of the sky as "Downtown Milky Way!" This starry wilderness is one of the richest parts of our own spiral galaxy. It's to wondrous places like this that some stargazers have "astral traveled" out of their bodies while viewing the heavens.

The Heart of the Whirlpool Galaxy

The heart of the famed Whirlpool Galaxy (M51) is seen here in all its glory. Its graceful spiral arms are outlined by regions where stars are still being born from its gas clouds. We view galaxies at differing orientations to us as they float in the ocean of intergalactic space—in this case, directly face on. This is how our own Milky Way would look as seen from the outside.

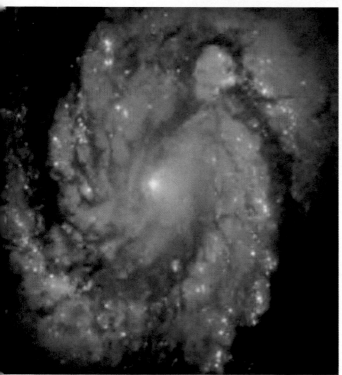

Spiral Galaxy M100

This lovely island of stars (M100) is tilted to our line of sight instead of being viewed face on as was the Whirlpool. Its majestic spiral arms laden with newborn suns and nebulosity can still be traced out as they swirl about the bright nucleus of the galaxy.

The Majestic Sombrero Galaxy (M104)

Seen nearly edge-on to us is the striking Sombrero Galaxy (M104), looking like some galactic Saturn. Huge star cities like this contain nearly a trillion suns, including thousands of individual globular clusters each hosting as many as a million stars! While most see a celestial Mexican hat here, others find a classic "flying saucer" cruising the abyss of intergalactic space. Although the Sombrero lies some twenty-eight million light-years from us (relatively close by, cosmically speaking), it can readily be seen in backyard telescopes—hat brim and all!

Entwined Star-Cities

Galaxies like this embracing pair (NGC 3314/NGC 3316) occasionally collide, but the stars within them do not—being so far apart that they pass each other like phantoms in the night, totally undisturbed. However, within the two galaxies the gas and dust do collide and heat up, producing regions of intense new star birth.

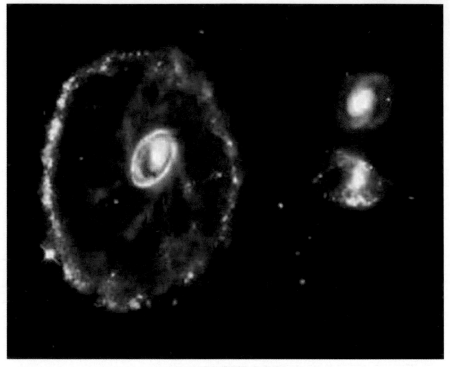

Cartwheel Galaxy

Galaxies, like stars themselves, typically occur in families ranging from just a few members, as seen in this image of the Cartwheel Galaxy and its companions, to as many as 10,000 in colossal superclusters.

A "Zoo of Galaxies"

A supercluster of galaxies lying some twelve billion light-years from us near the edge of the observable universe! The Hubble site refers to this image as a veritable "Zoo of Galaxies" due to the many different sizes and types of island universes it shows. As you gaze in wonder upon this spectacle, realize that you're not only looking twelve billion light-years out into space—but also twelve billion years *back into time!*

> in which the material consciousness may become cogni-
> zant of any being—being in the sense of an existent fact.
>
> 900-348

The reader may well ask what are we to take from the various read-ings quoted above on ethereal bodies and their celestial sojourns from the standpoint of modern astronomy itself—from what my late friend and mentor, astronomer Carl Sagan, called a "cosmic perspective"? The author has no doubt that sojourn experiences outside of our earthly bodies are real aspects of the universe we live in. And as we'll see else-where, such sojourns may help prepare us for our eventual return to the heavens from which we sprang. But I also strongly suspect there's more to this than meets the eye—that, as mentioned earlier, there's some "physicality" involved in visits to these other worlds.

For starters, we have only to think of the resurrected Christ, whose body wasn't entirely spiritual (Scripture tells us that He both ate and drank in the presence of His disciples—on the beach and in the upper room, respectively) and at the same time not entirely physical either (He walked on water and through walls). And then, of course, we have the many documented near-death experiences (NDEs) of people being outside of their bodies after "clinically dying" following heart attacks, accidents, or surgery. I've had the pleasure of speaking on the same program at several A.R.E. conferences with Dr. Raymond Moody, M.D., Ph.D., world-renowned for his pioneering work in this field. My contri-bution was sharing the many little-known benefits of stargazing—one of them being the out-of-body experiences (OBEs) or "astral travel" ex-perienced by both amateur and professional astronomers as they com-mune with the cosmos. I personally know many of these people; while their bodies were seated at the eyepieces of their backyard or observa-tory telescopes, their inner essence—their soul or spirit—was suddenly "out there" among the planets and stars and galaxies! This is something that the author has also experienced in my more than 20,000 hours of observing the heavens with the unaided eye, binoculars, and telescopes. And you can too, by making the amazing "photon connection" that's described later!

There's at least one reading in the Cayce material that hints at bridging the gap between the physical and spiritual realms of reality:

> These are the environs within the earth's activity in and about this present solar system, which is only a part or parcel of the great whole of the divine universe.
>
> Yet, as known and experienced by the application of the entity itself in the analyzing of same, there are the energies in each atom even of the physical body that are the shadows of the whole universe.   633-2

There are those who wonder if Edgar Cayce had a sense of humor while in the trance state. He did—and here's a wonderful example involving sojourns:

> (Q) Have I had an incarnation on the planet Jupiter?
> (A) In that environ, yes.
> (Q) Is it possible to secure a reading regarding conditions and my sojourn, if any, on that planet?
> (A) If you can understand Jupiterian environs and languages, yes. [!]   826-8

Those seeking a good reference to the various bodies making up our Sun's family should consult *The New Solar System*, edited by J. Kelly Beatty, Carolyn Petersen, and Andrew Chaikin (Sky Publishing and Cambridge University Press, 1999). It provides a wonderful overview of what we know about the physical conditions of our planetary neighbors from thirty scientists and is illustrated with marvelous spacecraft images of these worlds. Although this fourth edition is now some eight years old, the information it contains is still quite timely and enlightening. For those readers wanting to keep up with the very latest findings in this field, the Internet offers a veritable flood of up-to-the-minute information on all members and aspects of the solar system.

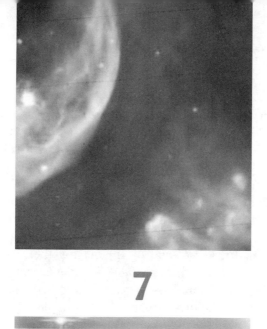

7

Gravity, Relativity, and Cosmology

QUANTUM PHYSICS AND CREATION

As mentioned earlier, while Edgar Cayce didn't use the word "cosmology" as such in the text of any of his readings, there's no question he was psychically tapping into its heady domain in speaking about multiple universes, other dimensions, and the vibratory nature of reality long before mainstream science itself did! He definitely did discuss gravity and the "relativity of force" (as he called it) in quite a number of his readings, some of which reveal profound insights into the nature of physical reality. An example of this is seen in the following discussion of the force of gravity and its role in forming new worlds:

> (Q) In occult chemistry it is given that force was begun in the interstices or bubbles in space and therefore space is the negation of force or matter. This being so . . .
>
> (A) [Interrupting] This is just what has been explained

here, in how these negations are formed in that as is called a bubble or becomes a sphere, in its attractibility to the forces as are in constant formation within our own sphere, see? That's the creation of worlds that's the creation as is kept in force, see?

(Q) [Continuing] This being so, gravity drawing everything to the center according to density, there comes a position from without a planet where space and lightest etheric matter meet—and the planet together with its atmosphere revolve through space. The planet, consisting of all degrees of vibrations—even to lightest etheric matter—have no relationship to space. An example somewhat similar on objective plane can be given as to the passage of etheric matter through what we term as solid substance. Is this theory correct? Gravity acting through space on everything has no action on space itself?

(A) That's the atomic theory! That is the theory as is seen—not theory, but the actual conditions as exist, as has been given and shown here in the activity of how forces build in their radiation without the application of space (as physically known), and how that there is the radiation through the forces as they move about one another.

195-57

What's so remarkable in this exchange is that not only does it give an accurate description of the creation process itself, but it also hints strongly that it involves the "quantum fluctuations" in the so-called vacuum of space which physicists and cosmologists are now convinced is the energy source for all of creation! Let's look now at some additional Cayce readings concerning the creation process itself:

The earth and the universe, as related to man, came into being through the *mind—mind—*of the Maker, and, as such, has its same being much as each atomic force multiplies in itself, or, as worlds are seen and being made in the present period, and as same became (earth we are speaking of) an abode for man, man entered as man, through the *mind* of the Maker, see?   900-227

That is, the kingdoms then being termed in the manner in which the conception may be gained better of this in earth's plane we are dealing with, alone, in this kingdom we find first, as the worlds created—and are still in creation in this heterogeneous mass as is called the outer sphere, or those portions as man looks up to in space, the mists that are gathering—what's the beginning of this? In this same beginning, so began the earth's sphere. The earth's sphere, with the first creation in the mind of the Creator, has kept its same Creative Energy, for God is the same yesterday, today and forever, and same in one creation creates that same in the other creation. One keeps right on through with the other, see?   900-340

In the beginning there was the force of attraction and the force that repelled. Hence, in man's consciousness he becomes aware of what is known as the atomic or cellular form of movement about which there becomes nebulous activity. And this is the lowest form (as man would designate) that's in active forces in his experience. Yet this very movement that separates the forces in atomic influence is the first cause, or the manifestation of that called God in the material plane!

Then, as it gathers of positive-negative forces in their activity, whether it be of one element or realm or another, it becomes magnified in its force or sources through the universe.

Hence we find worlds, suns, stars, nebulae, and whole solar systems *moving* from a first cause.   262-52

"And we may conclude likewise that this is the basis of

time, space, the universe. We do not see God because God
entirely obliterates self in incessant effort for good everywhere. If we look into the sprouting crops, the restless
ocean waves, the stars twinkling in the night, the puppies
and children playing, the application of electricity and
steam we see constant activity. We must understand, then,
that one of the attributes of the universe is activity. The
eternal hills of earth, the gaseous mass of the nebulae seem
changeless, but investigation of other worlds and nebulae
in differing stages of growth reveal that all are constantly
active."   (1341-1 Reports)

These amazing readings cover the entire scheme of creation from
atoms to stars and galaxies! Note especially Cayce's reference to "the
mists that are gathering" and to the "nebulae" and "nebulous masses."
This is indeed is how galaxies formed following the initial spark of creation in the Big Bang—from out of the swirling mists, and then how
stars and subsequently their planets condensed out of the nebulae
within the galaxies themselves. Incidentally, this is a process that's still
ongoing today. Stars are being born, evolving (over incredibly long lifetimes typically measured in the billions of years), dying—and being "reborn" as new stars form in part from the "ashes" of the old ones. (And
this is happening right now as you read this!)

Gravity and Antigravity

Edgar Cayce's most famous and in–depth reading regarding gravity,
vibration, and the relativity of force was given to an inventor who was
working on a perpetual motion motor. Here are some fascinating excerpts from this exchange ("GC" being Gertrude Cayce and "EC" Edgar
Cayce):

GC: You will have before you the body and enquiring
mind of [195], present in this room. You will have the
statement of law of relativity, also the explanation of the

theory and its application as applied to [4666] Motor; also a copy of reading given by Edgar Cayce concerning [4666] Motor, [4665-13, given September 24, 1928], all of which entity holds in his hand. You will answer the questions I will ask relative to law of relativity of force, its application, the interpretation of reading 4665-13 and the application of law on [4666] Motor.

EC: Yes, we have the body, the enquiring mind, [195]—this we have had before. Also there have been various phases of the law of relativity of force touched upon in various experiences, as have been presented. There are *many* varied conditions as are acted upon by this law that are perceptible to man's experience, yet have so far been little understood. The greater field as seen, so far, has been in that of chemical reaction, as has been studied by many. In some of the various theories, in some of the more closely allied manifestations, some have ferreted out the various forms in certain fields as appear in their experience; yet without understanding just what has taken place.

Now, with this dissertation in the beginning, as is seen, where the vibratory force—or the vibratory *theory*—is correlated *with* that of the various forms, then we begin to understand what is meant by relativity of force—or as will be seen in the various demonstrations of that that may be put into activity *through* this relativity of force—there will be the necessity of coining other words, as it were, to express just what is meant; for one may say relativity of force and it covers a multitude of sins, ideas, or of actual *force in action!* One may say gravity—and who understands just what is meant? It, the gravity, relative in its force to that of the combination of forces with *their* relative forces, see? Ready for questions . . .

(Q) Page 1, lines 1 to 5, would not each force be in a relativity to space also? Word the statement.

(A) Each force, each vibration, in its relative position to

that of space, or time, as is necessary in the *activity* of the generated force.

(Q) Can you give a short statement of general law of relativity of force?

(A) This may be better *manifested* than *stated*.

(Q) Page 1, lines 16 to 28, is statement as to resultant vibrations, also as to evolution, correct?

(A) As far as the *theory,* or as far as the actual fact of *vibratory* force and evolution, *correct.* As for application into mechanical forces, not *wholly* correct—but these become a portion of the same in activity. Now we find here, see [195]—this: The thing may be one thing standing still and an entirely different thing in vibratory forces in motion, see?

(Q) Are there any suggestions here?

(A) That just why, as has been stated, this may be demonstrated better than stated—yet when demonstrated there may be coined words necessary to mean just what is attempted to be *expressed.* For you see, that in common usage—Force, Vibration, Gravitation, Centralization, Centrifugal Force, Vibratory Force, Perpendicular, Angular, or in the various phases or forces—these merely present to the idea of the individual of certain positions, when relativity takes them *all*, see? . . .

(Q) Page 3, line 21, everything is vibratory—is . . .

(A) Absolutely correct!

(Q) Page 5, table of vibration—these are considered negative vibrations. What are positive vibrations? How would they be explained?

(A) How would one explain the differentiation between time in night and in day? How would one explain the differentiation in the activity of forces when there is a vibratory force set in a cellular force, and one is set in an oval or oblong force—which perpetrates, or penetrates, that force which produces or generates force as in its activity? In a negative force, as is seen in what has ordinarily or commonly in alchemy been called nightside. That as is of positive force is that as of the active force in its action, see? Now we have this demonstrated here in motor—here, with motor: In the various turns of the cams about the central portion of the drum, see? We have, when these in their turn are in opposition a negative force, see? *Now,* when they begin—by their turning over to become in a positive act—then you see the difference in them. Hence that as has been said as respecting the small end or the large end being in the radial force of that necessary to produce a positive, or an *active* rather than a negative—for if the negative becomes as powerful as the activity of the force in the positive, then we only begin and soon run down. Where does the difference in this, as from that as has been seen in ordinary balance, then begin? A balance is a negative force—as you would see from a scale—weigh so much—balance, see? Now in this we have the activity of gravitation, added to that force which keeps this in action, see? This constant action of gravitation, which is a portion *of* the force as of universal forces, which keeps all in its balance. See, it applies not only as right here—it applies right there, *everywhere*—in space, out of space, carries through in every form. What's the differentiation in the various forms? on which we could give a dissertation—But in the activity of this presented, as applied to that being brought by the gravitation, as indicated in this and the understanding its action—Water and air are necessary in a material demonstration, see? for they are in all, of all, and through all . . .

(Q) Page 6, lines 8 to 9, what are the various elements going to make up the force as applicable to elements in any generated force?

(A) Elements of the active principle in that called *now* generated energy, or the breaking of the vibratory unit to begin its expansion in force. As is in gravitation. In gravitation— *commonly* known—is that everything sinks to a common center, or is *drawn* to a common center; while that as is expanded is the positive energy in opposite relation to that force drawing. One goes up, the other we say goes down—as you would commonly express it. This is a very crude way, to say one goes up and one goes down—because it continues a circular motion in its activity, in this force . . .

(Q) In Reading 4665-13, Par. 7-A, lines 15 to 18, would force of gravity be considered to have elements in octave of density, and these in relativity to same forces of the object in question?

(A) That's the explanation! That is, now you have the correct line, see, as to how the octave of forces—Now let this apply not only to what is *commonly* considered as octave (meaning vibration thrown off as a sound), but as an octave or a vibration as would be set in motion by this very activity *of* the gravitation in its activity—as pushes up as well as pushes down. Not until you have overcome gravitation. Now you are beginning to understand the law of gravitation. So as the raising power, there must be the opposite power, see? We say everything goes up is bound to come down. When we begin to understand these, then we begin to see how the vibratory force is the active principle all radiates from. What is gravitation? The centralization of vibratory force, ready to be changed in power by non-activity, see?   195-54

This reading contains such deeply profound insights into the nature of gravity that it must be read many times before its full import can be absorbed and appreciated. And there's more about the nature of gravity and antigravity given in this later reading to the same individual, as well as two additional ones to other people:

(Q) Page 3—lines 1 to 8—["Consider Gravity—This applies right here, there and everywhere. This, too, may be considered a negative force, for it tends to balance the positive forces. Gravitational forces are vibratory forces and might be defined as the centralization of vibratory forces ready to change into power by non-activity."] Is gravity a negative force? How could this be better explained here?

(A) Gravity in this *sense*—as explained in that, in the activity that becomes passive in its force—gravity becomes the negative force, see? even as is illustrated.

195-70

In the beginning there was the force of attraction and the force that repelled. 262-52

(This reading is cited more fully above under the section on creation.)

Before that we find the entity was in the Atlantean land when there were the preparations of those things that had pertained to the ability for the application of appliances to the various elements known as electrical forces in the present day; as to the manners and ways in which the various crafts carried individuals from place to place, and what may be known in the present as the photographing from a distance, or the fields of activity that showed the ability for reading inscriptions through walls—even at distances, or for the preparations of the elevations in the various activities where there was the overcoming of (termed today) the forces of nature or gravity itself; and the preparations through the crystal, the mighty, the terrible crystal that made for the active principles in these, were a portion of the activity of the entity in that experience. 519-1

Note that all of the above readings talk about gravity as being a negative as well as a positive force—that it can repel as well as attract. And the last one actually mentions overcoming the force of gravity. These references certainly strongly support the existence of antigravity, for negative gravity *is* antigravity! The first reading also references gravity as being "octaves" of vibration or density, and the mysterious "nightside" forces (discussed below). Amazingly, all of these profound concepts found in the Cayce material are an integral part of the very latest findings in both theoretical physics and observational cosmology!

Nightside Forces

In Albert Einstein's early theoretical work on relativity, he found evidence in his equations that the universe was expanding (long before it was actually shown to be doing so by Edwin Hubble and others). In addition, they showed that there was a mysterious repulsive force at work that was overcoming the gravitational attraction that should have been causing the expansion to slow down, and eventually to stop and reverse itself. The complex mathematics indicated instead that this "antigravity" force was actually causing the expansion to accelerate with time and distance. This was all so unbelievable—even to a mind like Einstein's—that he introduced into his equations a "fudge factor," known as the "Cosmological Constant," to give a steady-state, non-expanding universe! Later in life, this great genius admitted to this being his "greatest blunder," for it had been shown conclusively by then that the universe was, indeed, expanding.

However, it has only been in the past several years, long after Einstein's death, that astronomers and cosmologists have found definite observational evidence that there is an antigravity force affecting the cosmos at large. It's well known today that less than 5% of the universe is visible to our eyes and instruments—that the other 95% is made up of "dark matter" and "dark energy." (There's nothing ominous in the use of the term "dark." It simply means that we can't see it.) The former accounts for about 20% of the total and is made up of some exotic invisible form of matter beyond that with which we're familiar. The remaining 70% consists of dark energy, which is what's causing the expansion of the universe to accelerate.

Was the ever–amazing Edgar Cayce referring to dark energy in mentioning the nightside forces of nature? The author (among others) strongly suspects that he was! If this is indeed the case, then as indicated in the following readings there actually were entities in ancient times who not only knew about this "fifth fundamental force," which dark energy is now considered to be, but (like antigravity) were able to put it to use:

> In the one before this we find in that period when known as Alta, in Atlantis. The entity among those who were of the highest development in the material application of these forces as pertain to the *nightside* of life, or the ability to apply that of forces not at present used in many ways for man's own use   2913-2

> In the one before this we find in that land known as Poseida, during those periods when man used all the forces in nature in the applying of same, whether to material forces or to mental. The entity was then among those of the rulers in the land, in the name Asmeelidkon. In this experience the entity lost *and* gained, for turning much of that understood of the nightside to those of secular in the experience brought much that was misunderstood.
>
> 1924-1

> In the one before this we find in that land known as Atlantis. The entity then was of the Poseidans, and gaining in repute of the abilities of the entity . . . using nightside of the influences in earth's plane brought destructive forces *to* self through the misapplication of power.   220-1

> In the one before this we find in that land known as Atlantean land, in that period when the peoples were

> coming to those conditions of the applications of the
> nightside of the laws as related to the governing of the
> universal forces, that might be applied to mechanics or to
> those of the necessities of peoples.   1714-1

Einstein and Relativity

Let's now turn our attention to what the Edgar Cayce readings had to
say about the concepts of relativity, space, and time. The term "relativity
of force" which was frequently used (as in reading 195–54 above) may
well have hidden within it subtle elements of Einstein's Theory of Relativity, but without alluding to the many bizarre relativistic effects for
which the theory is so famous today. And yet, the readings certainly
were aware of Einstein and his work.

> The entity builded in that of setting up the first study of
> how that the square of the one equal in the square of the
> other, as related to numbers and the *positions* of numbers
> as related to the stars in the universe, and the relation of
> one to another. The entity will *easily* understand Einstein's
> theory. Few would!   256-1

Cayce was also specifically asked about the subject of relativity on a
number of occasions:

> (Q) Explain in detail the law of relativity.
> (A) This law of relativity we find, as has been given, relates
> to the law as was set in motion in the beginning, when the
> Universe as a whole came into existence. As related to the
> mind, and to the earth conditions, we find first beginning
> with that of the earth in its position, with the other ele-
> ments about same. These became the law of the relative
> position regarding the spheres, and as there begun the
> lowest form of the animal and mineral, and vegetable,
> forces in the earth, we begun with all relative condition

> regarding those conditions from other spheres, and their
> relations to same.   900-24

In another attempt at explaining relativity, Cayce actually indicated
that the concept of relativity was known to certain individuals as far
back as ancient Egypt!

> As an illustration (this merely illustrating, now): It is hard
> for an individual, no matter how learned he may be, to
> conceive of the activities that exist only three miles above
> the earth. Why? Because there are no faculties within the
> individual entity in the present *capable* of conceiving that
> which is not represented within his individual self.
> Yea—but the individual of that period [Egypt] was not
> so closely knit in matter. Thus the activities of the realms
> of relativity of force, relativity of attraction in the universe,
> *were* an experience of the souls manifesting in the earth at
> that period, see?   281-42

Time and Space

Finally, we come to the provocative subjects of time and space (or
"space-time," as physicists and cosmologists call it). Let's again look to
the readings themselves to see what Edgar Cayce's insights were on
these key concepts of the cosmos:

> (Q) Are time and space concepts that exist outside of
> physical consciousness?
> (A) No. For the physical consciousness is an activity that
> uses such, as the divisions of space and time. And in
> patience only may ye become aware of the concept of
> either.   262-123

> For with the subconscious forces, we find that called the
> measure of space and time disappears, and the necessity is

for a material life to divide such into units called space and
time. See?   137-8

Then, as applying same, the entity finds that the whole
lesson, then, is that as has been given. All matter is as one
matter. All time as one time, and the various conditions as
are presented in that of the material plane, is as to the rate
of its vibratory force as is set in motion, and its portion of
that first Creative Energy that impels its own propagation,
in time, in space, in the material form and manner, and is
of man's—the highest created Creative Energy in the
material plane—the set spaces by man.   900-306

In considering such information, much—and much
more—might be given, or sought, as to how far-reaching
in space (time) is the information or the effects or benefits
from such reaching, in its range or scope of activity.
                                                     254-68

When it is the Life source, it is recorded upon space and
time—and is that which is to be kept against that day; for
time and space are as the evolution upon which the forces
of the divine make for that change that brings same into
the experiences of those souls who seek to become one
with the Creative Energies.   254-95

Thus we find His intervention in man's attempt throughout the eons of time and space. For these (time and space)
become portions of this three-dimensional plane. And
what is the other? Time, Space, Patience!   262-114

Or, to put in other terms, as has been given, the records of
time and space—present and future—are upon those films
that lie between time and space, and they become attuned
to those forces of the Infinite as the cells of the body

become attuned to the music of the realms of light and
space and time.   275-39

The Spirit ye worship as God has *moved* in space and time
to make for that which gives its expression; perhaps as
wheat, as corn, as flesh, as whatever may be the movement
in that ye call time and space.   281-24

Yet the entity itself sees, and is being taught, and is study-
ing, the records that are written in nature, in the rocks, in
the hills, in the trees, in that termed the genealogical log of
nature itself. Just as true, then, is the record that the mind
makes upon the film of time and space in the activities of
a body with its soul that is made in the image of the Maker;
being then spirit, in its form, upon the records *in* time and
space.

   As there may not be seen with the visible eye the growth
in animal, vegetable or mineral kingdoms, neither may
there be seen the growth in the soul, save by and through
the activities of a body-mind through channels known as
sense or intellect, or by drawing the comparisons in self
through what is termed space or time—and upon these are
the records of a soul's activity made.   487-17

How, it may be asked, do you arrive at such conclusions
from the entity's sojourn in those environs as indicated?
By what the entity did in those environs with the abilities
or knowledge that the entity had in its soul development
during such a sojourn. From what, then, do you gather
such information? Where are the records kept? Upon what
are they recorded? Upon the etheric wave in time and
space. That's what you are looking for, [490]! You'll find it!
   This film—in this film is the difference between the
movement *of* the atomic force about its center and the
impression that is made *upon* those passing *between* light

and heat, not darkness, for darkness may not exist where light has found its way. Though you may not be conscious or aware of its existence, its rays from the very records of time and space turn their emanations to give to a finite mind the dimensions themselves.   490-1

That upon the film of time and space, or that between time and space, makes or carries the records of the activities and thoughts of individuals in their sojourn through any realm of experience.   559-7

These do not mean the same in the varied spheres, but their activity is such that names—as has been given—so confine that they make confusion; for names are setting metes and bounds—and to this edge and to that edge, which *does not* exist! any more than time, space . . .826-8

(Q) Would you advise that I continue my work relative to music?
(A) As an example of the unison and rhythm of life, yes. As that which may supply oft that which bridges space and time, well.   1135-1

In the reading or interpreting of the records that are written, or that are impressions upon what we call time and space:
    We find that with patience we may learn of same, that—being forewarned—we may be forearmed; and thus see ourselves as we have recorded same upon that manifestation of Creative Forces or Energies *as* time and space.
    Time and space are occupied or are peopled with the elements, or spheres, that become activities for souls or entities in their journey through time and space . . .
                                                1597-1

For, while time and space are literal only to the consciousness of the finite mind, they are a part of the experience in materiality; and the presentations of same then should be of creative forces—as time, space, patience.   2000-3

(Q) How may I project a counterpart of my conscious awareness to any given place desired and comprehend or even take part in events there?
(A) Read what we have just been giving. This is an explanation of how. For it takes first spirit and mind form, and may be aware of the elements in space. For time and space are the elements of man's own concept of the infinite and are not realities as would be any bodily element in the earth—as a tree, a rose, a bird, an animal, as even a fellow being.   2533-8

God moved, the spirit came into activity. In the moving it brought light, and then chaos. In this light came creation of that which in the earth came to be matter; in the spheres about the earth, space and time; and in patience it has evolved through those activities until there are the heavens and all the constellations, the stars, the universe as it is known—or sought to be known by individual soul-entities in the material plane.   3508-1

(Q) [69]: Is the Celestial Sphere a definite place in the Universe or is it a state of mind?
(A) When an entity, a soul, passes into any sphere, with that it has builded in its celestial body, it must occupy—to a finite mind—space, place, time. Hence, to a finite mind, a body can only be in a place, a position.   5749-4

As this came about, it was necessary for their own awareness in the *spheres* of activity. Thus realms of systems came into being; as vast as the power of thought in attempting to

understand infinity, or to comprehend that there is no
space or time.   5755-2

When the heavens and the earth came into being, this
meant the universe as the inhabitants of the earth know
same; yet there are many suns in the universe—those even
about which our sun, our earth, revolve; and all are moving toward some place—yet space and time appear to be
incomplete.
        Then time and space are but one.   5757-1

The many profound ideas contained in the above readings amazingly concur with the very latest theoretical thinking—in particular, that
time and space are intimately related and that they are constructs of the
human mind. When Edgar Cayce said over and over again that "mind is
the builder," he must have realized that this includes the very cosmos
itself!

Ahead of His Time

Our discussion of Einstein has moved the author to close this chapter
with a letter that Edgar Cayce received in 1943 from a woman who had
read about him in Thomas Sugrue's classic *There Is a River*, which had just
been released the year before. It provides insight into how people with
extraordinary abilities such as Cayce's are often ignored or shunned,
and how far ahead of their time they may be—typically resulting in
their gifts being a "mixed blessing" for themselves (and often for their
families as well):

> "The book made me angry, too. It gave me that feeling I so
> often get when various issues, national and social, stir me
> so much I want to shout from the housetops and wake
> people up and make them see the light. I felt that way about
> you. I wanted to tell the world about you. I wanted to take
> the scientists and the doctors and shake the daylight out of

> them and say 'Are you so blind, so prejudiced that you
> cannot accept a truth when it is put right before your
> stupid noses?' Why are people so afraid to break away
> from the conventional beliefs? They believe an Einstein
> who got his gifts from God and they won't believe you.
> Well, I guess you answered that question yourself—man
> isn't ready for it and like other men with great gifts—you
> came too soon."   (3299-1 Background)

Those wishing to explore further the heady material covered in this chapter can do no better than read (and re-read!) the following two modern classics. One is Stephen Hawking's *A Brief History of Time* (Bantam Books, 1988). Hawking is the brilliant British mathematician and theoretical physicist from Cambridge University, who is widely regarded as the Einstein of today.

The other is *Black Holes and Time Warps: Einstein's Outrageous Legacy* (W.W. Norton, 1994) by Kip Thorne, one of the world's leading experts on gravity, relativity, and cosmology.

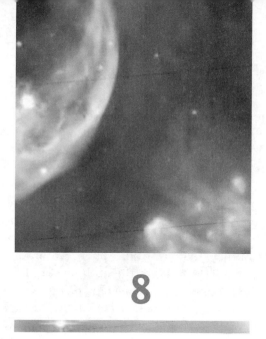

8

Achieving Our Cosmic Destiny

CHILDREN OF THE STARS

All of us living on Planet Earth are truly "children of the stars" (or "star children," as some prefer to call themselves), for as we've seen we are literally made of stardust! Hydrogen is the primordial element originating in the Big Bang itself (prompting the famed Harvard astronomer Harlow Shapley to state in 1958, "In the beginning was the Word, and the Word was hydrogen."). Except for it, all of the elements in your body were created *inside of exploding stars* eons ago! This includes the calcium in your fingernails, teeth, and bones; the iron that's coursing though your bloodstream as you read this; the carbon making up the cells of your body; and even the potassium in your brain that allows you to think and understand this book.

Earlier we examined some of the Cayce readings concerning planetary, astrological, and astral sojourns, and we also explored the subject of life elsewhere in the universe and our intense fascination with the night sky. As mentioned, we seem in a sense to have been genetically programmed to return to our source—to that cosmos from which the very elements that we are made of came. As the sea calls to so many of us here on Earth, so too do the stars in the heavens above. The philosopher Eric Hoffer explained this as " . . . a kind of homing impulse—we are drawn to where we came from." Interestingly, we are told by the Cayce readings to "Seek then, ye, in understanding as to where, why, from what source, there may be gained the experiences of an entity, a soul, through its journeys in this the odic sphere, or through that known as this solar system." (254-68) What the author would like to suggest here (and something I personally believe) is *that the various sojourns described by Edgar Cayce have "genetically disposed" us to return to those worlds in our physical bodies where our souls have previously traveled!*

Citizens of the Universe

In the November/December 2006 issue of *Venture Inward* magazine, Mark Thurston wrote in an article entitled "Citizens of the Universe" an opening paragraph that is so pertinent to what has just been said that it's worth quoting:

> "Looking up at a star-filled sky, one can't help but wonder if there is life 'out there.' Modern-day fascination with science fiction (e.g., *Star Trek*) and the possibility of extraterrestrial life add to the mystery. And as soon as we introduce the ideas of reincarnation and planetary sojourns (as Cayce called our journeys between physical incarnations), it's not such a big step to start wondering, 'Are those star systems the very places where my own soul has ventured in the past or will some day travel?'"

The great French popularizer of astronomy, Camille Flammarion, used a similar term—"Citizens of Heaven"—to describe those of us who are stargazers. Others have called us "Naturalists of the Night," "Harvesters of Starlight," "Star Pilgrims," and even "Time Travelers"—the farther we look out into space the farther back into time we're seeing. (If you are reading this book and are not already a member of this celestial fraternity, you simply *must* join us!) There is at least one reference by the Edgar Cayce readings to becoming a citizen of the universe: "[Humankind] may become, with the people of the universe, ruler of any of the various spheres through which the soul passes in its experiences." (281-16)

Our Cosmic Bodies

The reader is now asked before going any further to take a few minutes to review the section on astral travel; the discussion about the personification of the stars; and finally, John Van Auken's beautifully written piece from his *Personal Spirituality* newsletter, quoted earlier, about our being regarded as "godlings" and as "stars in the heavens of God's mind" by the ancient Egyptians. Meditating on the implications of their collective contents should leave no doubt in your mind that we truly do possess both Earth–bound physical bodies and cosmic celestial ones.

Considering this, hopefully you are prepared to accept the prophetic and profound truth of the following words from author William Fix: "We are still reaching for the stars, even as the Egyptians reached for them forty centuries ago. But we are just rediscovering that our starships are within us; a subtle body that can pass through matter and fly with the speed of thought is indeed a vehicle in which man could cross cosmic distances." Indeed, those stargazers who have had—and continue to have—out-of-body experiences while observing the heavens will tell you that this is something they have actually already done!

Here now are a number of readings by Edgar Cayce concerning our celestial or cosmic bodies:

> There are bodies celestial, bodies terrestrial.   900-59

> First, let it be understood there is the pattern in the material or physical plane of every condition as exists in the cosmic or spiritual plane, for things spiritual and

things material are but those same conditions raised to a different condition of the same element—for all force is as of one force. _____   5756-4

Considereth thou that Spirit hath its manifestations, or does it *use* manifestations for its activity? The Spirit of God is aware through activity, and we see it in those things celestial, terrestrial, of the air, of all forms. And *all* of these are merely manifestations! The Knowledge, the understanding, the comprehending, then necessitated the entering in because it partook of that which *was* in manifestation; and thus the *perfect* body, the celestial body, became an earthly body and thus put on flesh . . . When the earth became a dwelling place for matter, when gases formed into those things that man sees in nature and in activity about him, then matter began its ascent in the various forms of physical evolution—in the *mind* of God! The spirit chose to enter (celestial, not an earth spirit—he hadn't come into the earth yet!), chose to put on, to become a part of that which was as a command not to be done! Then those so entering *must* continue through the earth until the body-mind is made perfect for the soul, or the body-celestial again.   262-99

(Q) Is the Celestial Sphere a definite place in the Universe or is it a state of mind?
(A) When an entity, a soul, passes into any sphere, with that it has builded in its celestial body, it must occupy—to a finite mind—space, place, time. Hence, to a finite mind, a body can only be in a place, a position. An attitude, sure—for that of a onement with, or attunement with, the Whole. For, God is love; hence occupies a space, place, condition, and *is* the Force that permeates all activity.
                                            5749-4

... for, as is seen, the body physical has the attributes of the physical body. The body celestial or cosmic body has those attributes of the physical with the cosmic added to same, for all of hearing, seeing, understanding, becomes as *one*. Then there is that question arising, then, as to how the differentiation then in the cosmic plane. With the attempting to disseminate, divide these conditions, we find how or why the material body is unable to hear, see, gain the presence of such conditions in the cosmic, astral or celestial bodies—yet when the celestial body approaches this may come in any of the various forces as pertain to that manner in which the material consciousness may become cognizant of any being—being in the sense of an existent fact. Yet the very fact that all become as one, and the entity so communicating, so giving, is able to give the information to one that has laid aside that of the physical being so that the operation is through that condition in which the cosmic forces become as that builded in the soul body. The soul body being then that form in which the cosmic body is when absent from the physical being, and while a portion of the whole and all the attributes of the body being one *with* the whole, yet the ideal or I AM remaining with that which has been *builded* by the experiences of the soul through its *contact with* the various conditions in the astral, cosmic, celestial or through those same in the *fleshly* body. Hence we find how these various conditions may be communicated one with another.   900-348

·

Stargazing and the Photon Connection

Earlier in this chapter I invited the reader who is not already a stargazer to become one, for seeing the wonders of the heavens firsthand is the next best thing to actually being out there in a strictly physical sense, and also an ideal way to reconnect with our cosmic origins. And there are many other unsuspected benefits in personally communing with the cosmos. These include therapeutic relaxation using the stars as celestial mandalas to meditate upon; expansion of consciousness, as the most sublime and profound thoughts frequently come to stargazers during their nightly vigils under the sky (which many suspect is the result of tapping into the telepathic exchanges between other intelligences in the universe); and spiritual contact with the awesome Mind that lies behind creation at its grandest, for nature is truly pinnacled in the stars!

However, the benefit most intimately linked with this chapter's topic is the previously mentioned experience of many stargazers of having traveled outside of their bodies (or "astral traveled") while peering skyward. It turns out that there's actually an explanation for how such experiences can occur, examining them from the standpoint of astronomical science. It involves a profound but virtually unknown aspect of looking at the stars—something the author has called the "photon connection." (This name first appeared in my article, "Making the Photon Connection," published in the June 1994 issue of *Sky & Telescope* magazine—the world's leading astronomy periodical, read by both amateur and professional astronomers.)

This revolves around the fact that when we look at a celestial object like a star or nebula or cluster or galaxy or quasar, we are seeing it by the photons of light it is emitting. And as has been long known by science, photons have a very strange "dualistic" nature; they behave as both particles *and* waves—or as particles traveling in waves, as I like to think of it. This means that when I view one of the nearest quasars known as 3C–273 (which lies some two billion light–years from us) in the constellation Virgo through my telescope, I'm actually getting a piece of it on the retina of my eye. *Something that was once inside of it has traveled across the vastness of space and time and ended its journey inside of me!* No wonder stargazers have had such uplifting and inspiring thoughts while looking at the stars—and no wonder they have in many cases left their bodies to go there!

In the September/October 2002 issue of *Venture Inward*, the author published an article, "Divine Order in the Universe," which those having access to back issues of the A.R.E.'s membership magazine are urged to read. In it I quoted the following deeply moving lines from Dostoevsky's classic *The Brothers Karamazov*: "Oh! in his rapture he was weeping even over those stars, which were shining to him from the abyss of space, and he was not ashamed of that ecstasy. There seem to be threads from all those innumerable worlds of God, linking his soul to them, and it was trembling all over in contact with [these] other worlds . . . " Those "threads" may well be the connecting "photonic link" with our celestial or soul body—the famed "silver cord" of the mystics. In the author's opinion, this ties in beautifully with the various sojourns to other worlds discussed in so many of Edgar Cayce's readings and supports the fact that such sojourns did indeed actually happen!

As mentioned earlier, the reader may also have an opportunity to personally experience the thrill of astral travel by making the photon connection while viewing the stars. Here's just one way of doing it: On some dark (moonless) clear summer night, look up at the great billowy starclouds of our Milky Way Galaxy where it passes through the constellations Cygnus, Aquila, Scutum, and especially Sagittarius. (They are so obvious in places that many people have seen them but have mistaken them for storm clouds forming. But these are not rain clouds— they are massed *starclouds!*) Examine them using your unaided eye or, better yet, a pair of binoculars. When you come to the realization that the brighter stars in these clouds are closer to you than are the fainter ones—*that you are seeing layer upon layer of countless numbers of stars and sensing depth*—the Milky Way may suddenly jump right out of the sky at you as the three-dimensional starry pinwheel that it actually is!

It's here and in similar experiences that some stargazers have suddenly found themselves "out there" among the hosts of beckoning suns! While this typically lasts for just a few brief moments, I personally suspect it's a "sneak preview" of the sojourns Cayce mentioned—which in most cases lasted a "lifetime" for those to whom he gave past-life readings.

There exist a multitude of books and guides on all aspects of stargazing, but (quite sadly) very few of these discuss it from an aesthetic or spiritual perspective. Two that do (and that also happen to be two of the very best books ever written on the subject) are *The Soul of the Night* by professional astronomer Chet Raymo (Hungry Mind Press, 2003) and

Starlight Nights by famed amateur astronomer Leslie Peltier (Sky Publishing, 1999)—the discoverer of a dozen comets, among other amazing feats. Another "must" resource for any stargazer is one (or both) of the world's two leading astronomy magazines, *Sky & Telescope* and *Astronomy*. In addition to reporting on all the latest discoveries in the field, they provide superb monthly star and planet charts along with previews of exciting upcoming celestial events such as eclipses and meteor showers.

Our Cosmic Destiny

And so we come to the end of our cosmic journey. Edgar Cayce has been our psychic and spiritual guide, while the discoveries of modern physics, astronomy, and cosmology have served as our scientific guide. We've seen that we came from the stars—that our bodies are literally made of stardust. And the author (among countless others) is absolutely convinced that we're destined to return to the stars as part of our cosmic heritage and birthright. Some believe that this will be in the ethereal/soul/cosmic/celestial bodies that Cayce talked about, while others see this actually happening in our physical bodies. In either case, we're destined join the galactic community as representatives of our solar system and Planet Earth—a community that has been patiently waiting for us in the case of our Galaxy's oldest stars and their civilizations for *billions* of years! What an exhilarating prospect—especially for those of us who know (or at least suspect) that we have already been out there!

The author's favorite comment by Edgar Cayce concerning this awesome expectation, and one which provides a perfect summary of what this book has been all about, is:

> For, know that each soul, each entity, is so much a part of that universal consciousness as to cause those forces termed the planetary influences to be mis-shaped in their activity. For, the universe was brought into being for the purpose of being the dwelling place of the souls of God's children— of which birthright this entity is a part.   2396-2

Many visionaries have described this transition from Mortal Man/ Woman to Cosmic Man/Woman as "graduation day" for our species. Indeed it definitely shall be, as we move out into the cosmic deeps! For a preview of what it may be like, the reader is here referred to the hauntingly prophetic novels by Sir Arthur Clarke *Childhood's End* and *2001: A Space Odyssey* (Del Rey/Ballentine, 1953 and 1968, respectively). Sir Arthur was definitely looking into the future (as he has so often done) in these two visionary works.

I would like also to share a few lines here from Charles Edward Barns' long–out–of–print classic stargazing guide *1001 Celestial Wonders*. While these words were intended to describe the excited anticipation of look- ing skyward on a clear night, they could just as well apply to the won- drous anticipation of our transition as a race to the stars:

> Lo, the Star-lords are assembling
> And the banquet-board is set;
> We approach with fear and trembling,
> But we leave them with regret.

I, for one, am eagerly looking forward to achieving our cosmic des- tiny. Along with countless others who have moved on from their last earthy reincarnations, Edgar Cayce is surely waiting patiently for us on some world, in some form, out there among the lights in the night sky. I really can't wait to see him, because I want first of all to thank him personally for sharing his amazing psychic gift with us. And as an as- tronomer, I also have a couple of thousand questions to ask him about the cosmos!

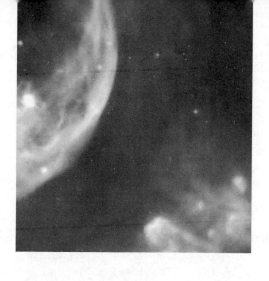

Appendix 1
Who Was Edgar Cayce?

EARLY LIFE

Edgar Cayce was born on a farm outside of Hopkinsville, Kentucky, on March 18, 1877, and was one of five children. As was typical of those times, many of his relatives lived nearby, and from all accounts, he had a rich and happy family life growing up. As a little child, Edgar had many imaginary playmates, and by the age of six or seven, he told his parents that he was having visions and talking to deceased relatives. Not unexpectedly, his family largely ignored him in such matters, attributing them to his very active and fertile imagination.

Cayce developed an interest in the Bible at a very early age, which was likely a result of the religious revivals sweeping the country at the time. It brought him great comfort, and he set himself the goal of reading it from cover to cover each year of his life. He also soon made up his mind that he would become a doctor and a minister, spreading the "Word" while healing the sick. This decision was supported by a vision he had when he was thirteen years old. A beautiful woman appeared to him and asked what he most wanted to do with his life. His response was that he wanted to help others, especially little children who were ill.

Soon after this, Edgar developed a talent that could not possibly be explained away by an overactive imagination—a photographic memory! He was able to sleep on top of his school books (and eventually any kind of book or paper, however complex) and repeat word-for-word their entire contents. For a time this uncanny ability helped him in his school studies but it eventually slowly disappeared. By then a teenager, Cayce had to quit school anyway to help with expenses, and he began working on his grandmother's farm.

The family eventually moved from the farm to the town of Hopkinsville itself, and Cayce found a job at a local bookstore. Within just a few months he met and fell in love with his soul mate, Gertrude Evans. They became engaged in March of 1897 and planned to get married once they were in a position to afford to have the family they both wanted. But by the following summer, Edgar had lost his job and moved to Louisville, Kentucky, in the hope of finding a good-paying position there. At Christmas, 1899, he went back to Hopkinsville to work with his father in the insurance business, becoming a traveling salesman. He was now well on his way to earning enough money to finally get married. But one day during this period, Edgar took a sedative to relieve a severe headache and in so doing developed a bad case of laryngitis that would not go away. Despite seeing several doctors, he was only able to communicate in whispers, and after several weeks of this, he had to relinquish his job as a salesman. Still unable to speak months later, he feared that he would never be able to talk again.

Cayce finally landed what proved to be an ideal position for himself back in Hopkinsville—that of a photographer's assistant at a local studio. Here he was close to both his family and his Gertrude, and with their loving support he could better deal with his seemingly incurable condition. And while he regretted never being able to finish his formal education to become the doctor and minister he dreamed of becoming, he found contentment in being back home with family and his bride-to-be.

It so happened that at the turn of the century hypnotism had become very popular and traveling shows demonstrating its powers visited many towns including Hopkinsville. On one of these occasions a hypnotist hearing about Cayce's laryngitis offered to attempt to cure him using the power of the subconscious mind. He put Edgar in a hypnotic trance and told him that he could talk normally again. And although he did so while under hypnosis, when he awakened his voice was gone. This was done several times with a post-hypnotic suggestion to awake having normal speech, but it didn't "take." Then a local man versed in hypnotism offered to try again. Under hypnosis he asked Edgar to explain to him what was actually causing the laryngitis and how to cure it. Cayce immediately replied, telling him of a physical condition involving lack of blood circulation to the affected area—and that it could be cured simply by a suggestion under hypnosis for it to increase. And indeed this worked! This amazing event occurred on March 31, 1901, and marked the beginning of the long series of Cayce's famed medical readings that covered a span of more than forty years.

Needless to say, Gertrude and Edgar's family were thrilled that he was able to speak normally once again. Now he could continue with his career as a photographer and plans to get married. He intended to give no further thought to hypnotism and trances—but the man who made his cure possible had other ideas, for he himself was suffering from a serious stomach ailment. He asked Cayce to go into a trance again and diagnose his problem. Skeptical, Cayce reluctantly agreed to try, reminding himself that it was due to this man that he could speak again. The "reading" he thus gave brought about an effective cure based on diet and exercise.

The Mission Begins

From this point on, there was no turning back. Edgar Cayce felt that he had been placed in a very difficult position. On one hand, he knew nothing about medicine or diagnosing illnesses, and the whole idea of giving readings while in a trance state seemed quite strange to him. But on the other hand, he now seemingly had a moral obligation to use his newly found remarkable abilities to help others if he possibly could. After much prayer and discussion with both Gertrude and his family, Edgar reluctantly agreed to continue giving readings under two conditions: First, if he ever said anything while in the trance state that might possibly prove harmful to those for whom the readings were given, the sessions would be stopped; and, second, he wanted people to know that he was first and foremost a photographer and not a psychic! His earnest desire was simply to lead a quiet normal life.

It was soon found that Cayce did not need to have the person for whom a reading was being given physically present, but only the name, location, and condition were required to effect a diagnosis. He himself was puzzled and even baffled by many of the readings upon seeing what had been written down during the trance, and he often frankly stated that he didn't understand a word about what he had said! But he resolved to continue giving readings and found it gratifying that he was able to help others through his gift. And in time, the scope of the readings expanded to include not just medical conditions but a host of other subjects, including reincarnation and past lives, astrological sojourns, dream interpretation, Earth changes, ancient civilizations, and even past and coming world events.

In addition to his work as a busy photographer and giving psychic readings, Edgar finally found time to marry Gertrude after an engagement of six years. This happy event occurred on June 17, 1903, following which the couple moved to Bowling Green, Kentucky, to set up housekeeping and to allow Cayce the opportunity of opening his own photography studio. Many events followed in the ensuing years, including the birth of their three sons, Hugh Lynn, Milton Porter (who died shortly after birth), and Edgar Evans, and two costly studio fires that left the Cayce's in serious debt.

As requests for readings continued to come in at an ever-increasing pace, Edgar finally decided to give up his photography business and concentrate on giving readings essentially full-time. While he gave his early ones without charge, he now began taking donations for them. However, very characteristically, he never refused to do a reading because of a person's inability to contribute something. As his fame spread, more and more people approached him for readings involving their illnesses. But the problem was that there was no one in the medical profession qualified and/or willing to carry out his treatment recommendations. So he began dreaming about founding a center or hospital where people could come both to get readings and to receive treatment from qualified doctors, nurses, and therapists. A number of financial backers who believed in Cayce's work were soon found who could make this dream a reality. Among the cities that they suggested for the hospital were Chicago and Dayton. But the readings stated repeatedly that it needed to be located in or near Virginia Beach, Virginia, on the Atlantic Ocean. Finally, a New York businessman for whom Edgar had given readings agreed to put up the money to build the hospital at that location. His name was Milton Blumenthal, and he continued to be actively involved with Cayce for a number of years thereafter.

Move to Virginia Beach

Edgar Cayce and his family—along with Gladys Davis, his trusted secretary who recorded most of his later readings—moved to Virginia Beach in September 1925. In 1927, the Association of National Investigators (not a group of criminologists!) was formed to research and experiment with the information contained in the Cayce readings. In November of the following year, the hospital itself was finally opened. People from all over the country came to the Beach for readings and treatment. Each patient was given a reading in which Cayce diagnosed their condition or illness, and then recommended treatment options ranging in scope from diet and exercise to homeopathic medicines and surgery. By 1930, the educational arm of the Cayce complex known as Atlantic University was opened. The hospital itself operated until late 1930, when the Great Depression brought with it the loss of financial backing, and it sadly closed the following February. The University continued operating until that Christmas. (It eventually reopened and today is a recognized institution, offering advanced degree programs in transpersonal studies and other subjects to students from far and wide.) Finally, in June 1931, the Association for Research and Enlightenment,

Inc.— better known as the A.R.E.—was formed to further study and disseminate the treasures contained within the Cayce readings. It still thrives today, more than three-quarters of a century later, to the immense benefit of the entire world. It is without question one of the leading lights in the transformation of human health and consciousness on this planet—a fitting memorial and lasting legacy to the man who simply wanted to help others.

Expanding Abilities and Growing Demands

In time, Edgar Cayce became ever more psychic, including in a waking state, as well. He once ran out of a room in sorrow because he knew that three of the men in it would be lost in battle during the War. He also developed the ability to see the auras surrounding people, which he used to deduce their physical and emotional conditions. There's a famous story that, in this case tragically, illustrates this. Edgar was about to step into an elevator full of people when he suddenly stepped back before the doors closed. The auras of the people in the elevator were *missing!* The elevator cable broke and it fell into the basement, killing everyone inside.

As Cayce's fame continued to spread, many skeptics (including reporters for national magazines) came to Virginia Beach to expose him as just a clever showman. But they soon became convinced that his psychic abilities were for real, and many ended up having readings done for themselves! One of those initially skeptical was the well-known religious writer Thomas Sugrue (who had been acquainted with Hugh Lynn Cayce in college). He came to prove for himself that Edgar Cayce was a fraud—but ended up instead accepting Cayce's psychic ability. Subsequently, Sugrue wrote the classic biography of the Sleeping Prophet entitled *There Is A River*. (This reminds the author of a very similar situation involving UFOs, in which a highly skeptical scientist, the noted astronomer J. Allen Hynek of *Close Encounters of the Third Kind* fame, ended up not only accepting the reality of the phenomenon but also actively researching it.)

At the height of World War II, Cayce was receiving an ever-increasing number of requests for readings, and he soon found himself booked nearly *two years in advance*! He was warned by family and close friends to limit his readings to two daily, but due to the huge backlog of requests, he was instead giving as many as eight a day. By early 1944, he began to grow weak from overwork. Despite the fact that his own readings told him to slow down and rest, he felt a deep obligation to help as many people as he possibly could. Sadly, this finally took its toll. By the fall of that year, he collapsed from exhaustion and suffered a stroke which left him partially paralyzed. He said that he would be "healed" by the first of the year, but as those close to him suspected, he really meant that he would transition by then. He died on January 3, 1945, at the age of 67. His devoted wife Gertrude, who had also been ill, followed him just three months later, on Easter Sunday.

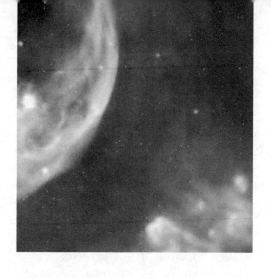

Appendix 2
The Language of the Cayce Readings

BY GINA CERMINARA, Ph.D.

Anyone who has ever had a reading from Edgar Cayce knows that the language in which it was couched was very often very hard to understand. The involved phrases and odd expressions are apparent even in the brief paragraphs that appear in [early A.R.E. publications]; and a person coming upon these passages for the first time might well wonder if it is not a case of making the waters muddy so that they may appear to be deep.

Such a suspicion is not unnatural; but any person who has made a careful, impartial, and thorough study of the material knows that it is quite unfounded. Through what one critic called the "rambling, redundant, ambiguous, and evasive verbal meanderings" there ran a current of high and genuine import. Thousands of people whose physical health has been transformed and whose psychological difficulties resolved by the contents of the readings will testify to this fact.

But the question remains: Why *was* the language so odd? Why the psychic double-talk? Why not come out and say, "This is a spade" instead of pussy-footing around with, "This as we find, has to do with not the consciousness in spirituality (as commonly conceived) but rather the consciousness in materiality, as condensed in what is known as, or called, in the present, an implement of spading, or a spade."

To this question we cannot give a complete authentic answer because we are not in possession of all the facts in the case. But we can draw some reasonable deductions from what the readings themselves have offered as explanation, and we can make an intelligent appraisal of all the facts as we know them, in connection with the phenomenon of language in general.

In the first place it must be recognized that Mr. Cayce was *not* a medium in the usual sense of the word. It was his own superconscious mind—highly developed and trained in past incarnations in Egypt and Persia—which, when the ordinary consciousness was laid aside in sleep, became active and was able to attune itself with whatever source was necessary to secure the information desired.

The sources upon which the soul-entity of Mr. Cayce should draw were several. These—as explained by the readings themselves—can be summed up as follows:

(1) the subconscious mind of Edgar Cayce himself;
(2) the subconscious mind of other individuals in the earth plane. (When a life reading was given, the information came in part from the subconscious of the one on whom the reading was given; this was also true, to some extent, in the case of the physical readings):
(3) the subconscious minds of discarnate entities in the spirit plane;
(4) the soul minds of higher masters;
(5) the Akashic records;
(6) The Universal cosmic consciousness.

Now it seems fairly clear that—whichever source he used to obtain his information, he was speaking from a point of view infinitely vaster and more intricate than the point of view of earth-plane man, and it is perhaps for this reason that a language difficulty arises. The choice of words is often labored; the phrases seem chosen from an odd and unusual angle—much like a photographic study taken from an angle and in a focus not ordinarily thought of.

Exactly what the language mechanism was has never been explained by the readings themselves, except for very fragmentary remarks to the effect that higher-dimensional realities can not easily be expressed in three-dimensional terms. This sounds reasonable. And piecing together what the readings themselves have said with the linguistic impressions one gathers on examining the readings, one arrives at some fairly satisfactory conclusions.

These impressions can be summarized as follows:

(1) the readings sound like a man speaking in a foreign language;

(2) they sound like a person from an ancient era trying to speak to a modern era;

(3) they sound like a highly educated person—or an academician—trying to make himself clear to the uneducated—or the non-academic.

The first impression—that of a man trying to speak in a foreign language—is very strong. One feels, primarily, as if a highly cultivated and benevolent philosopher of a very remote country, say China or Afghanistan, were attempting to speak in English—and the English language is notoriously difficult for foreigners. Native turns of speech, awkward use of idiom, flagrant mistakes of syntax and grammar, oddly combined with occasional perfection of syntax and grammar are typical of the speech of foreigners—who often use subjunctives and pronouns more accurately than we do ourselves, and consequently sound stilted in doing so.

Moreover the use of archaic expressions in the readings, such as "oft," "babe," "wilt," etc., suggest that the speaker is a foreigner not only in space but also in time. These out-moded forms of English may hark back to Mr. Cayce's early American incarnation; and characteristic ways of using certain words, such as "same" and "self" (as, for example, "the entity, remembering same, will make much progress," and "First analyze self") may be idiomatic in one of the ancient languages, either Egyptian or Persian, with which Mr. Cayce's soul–entity was once familiar.

The stiltedness of many passages in the readings give rise to still a third impression—namely, that of an individual educated far above the level of the person to whom he is talking, and attempting to talk down to the level of the second person. This offers both psychological and linguistic difficulties. Ph.D.'s and professors, for example (to say nothing of the writers of income tax laws and the Congressional Record) are notorious for their use of style incomprehensible to the majority. In some cases this may be due to affectation, or to that kind of social ineptitude that arises from many years of academic seclusion. But generally speaking, there is among this type of persons a genuine habituation to certain language constructions, which they can depart from only with great effort. The breadth, subtility and complexity of their thought is something to which the uneducated are not accustomed. The necessity, then, to make themselves intelligible to people whose outlook is innocent of ideological or technical preoccupations, and whose speech is rough and ready for the simple purposes of making a living, is often a difficult one.

The difficulty in self–expression which was obviously experienced by the giver of information in the readings seems quite comparable. They read like the speech of a man who because of the habitual grandeur of his thoughts, is clumsy when trying to speak at any level other than his own. And, aware of his own clumsiness, he becomes repetitious in the anxious effort to become clear.

Finally, it must be remembered that the readings were given from a point of view of an enlarged consciousness—that is to say, the source of information was conversant with many dimensions, and needed to condense what he knew into three–dimensional terms. This is a difficult thing for us to grasp, because we are all so completely imbedded in a three–dimensional consciousness that we can not conceive of realities of four, five, six, seven, and more dimensions. Yet both mathematicians and physicists, occultists and clairvoyants, assure us that higher dimensions *do* exist; and the readings themselves, as before indicated, often make reference to the fact.

By way of learning to appreciate the difficulty involved in compressing knowledge into narrower terms than those really adequate to describe it, one might try a little experiment. One might attempt to make a description of something, say the American flag, without using any words that contain the letter "r," on the assumption that you were talking to a person whose version of the English language contained no letter "r."

It seems a simple enough sort of assignment. Yet the moment you began to refer to the most basic features of the thing you would realize that you could use neither the words *stars* nor *stripes*. Your first task would be to find other ways of expressing those ideas. Not even *bars* could substitute for *stripes*, and perhaps *bands* would be the closest available equivalent. For *stars* you might begin to say, "five-pointed figures," and in the midst of it realize that *figures* would be incomprehensible to an "r"–less people; so you would settle on "five-pointed symbols of heavenly bodies."

Red would be your next preoccupation. You could neither say *darker* nor *deeper* shade of pink, but finally you would approximate the idea by saying "deep pink" or possibly (especially if you were familiar with the nail-polish ads of the country) "passion pink."

Your difficulties are not, however, now at an end. You can not say there are *thirteen* bands which *alternate* in *color*, nor can you remark that there are *forty*-eight stars which represent *forty*-eight states [in 1945] of the United States of *America*. Even *country* would be unavailable to you.

Devising circumlocutions for all these tabu—or, in a sense, non–existent words—you might finally emerge with a description something like this:

"The flag of the United States of the Continent of the West (that is, the land found by Columbus) consists of eight and five bands of white and a tint that might be called deep pink, passion pink, wine pink, that is to say, the tint of blood—a band of white and then a band of this tint. In the top left of the flag is a field of blue on which we see twenty and twenty-eight five-pointed symbols of heavenly bodies, each to stand as symbol of the twenty and twenty-eight states that make up the land."

This—as anyone who has ever read a Cayce reading will admit—

sounds extraordinarily like a reading—and its clumsiness very likely arises from the same basic cause. The readings, of course, need no apology. Their merit has been proven so many thousands of times in so many extraordinary cases that the genuineness of their clairvoyance can simply not be questioned. But it has seemed worthwhile to write this article in the interest of bringing out into the open a matter which, to some people at least, looms large as an obstacle to the full acceptance of the readings. For general publication purposes, indeed, it has become necessary to adopt careful editorial policies of simplification or clarification, in order that the message may be understandable by the majority; but even after this has been done, under rigorous supervision of Mr. Cayce's secretary, the language still retains a certain quaint flavor.

In this connection it is well to remember, however, that the substance, sincerity, or intrinsic value of a message can not always be judged by the language in which it is clothed. Some of the best writing in the civilized world, for example, is now being done in the field of advertising. The most poetic of prose—sensitive, direct, dynamic—is found in advertising copy, and frequently the pages of advertisements make more compact, interesting, and instructive reading than the text of the magazine itself. But oftener than not that magnificent writing is the cloak for a lying message, a hypocritical appeal, and a subtle, deliberate, and crassly self–interested playing upon the reader's sensibilities.

By all means use all your faculties of discrimination and critical judgment with regard to the Cayce readings. But do not permit the clumsiness of the language to deflect you from the genuine worth of their contents.

[Article originally printed in the December 1945 *A.R.E. Bulletin*, reprinted April 1966 in *The A.R.E. Journal*.]

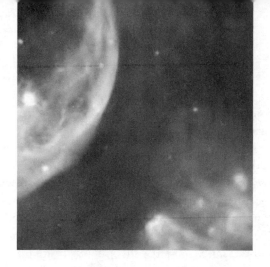

Appendix 3
The Akashic Records

What *was* the source that Edgar Cayce was tapping into when he gave the readings? He stated that the information they contained was actually derived from two primary sources. One was the subconscious mind of the person for whom he was giving the reading. The other (and apparently much vaster) source was the Akashic records, which are a cosmic recording, somehow written and stored in space and time, of every thought, word, and deed of every person who has ever lived on this planet! As Cayce entered into his trance state, he was no longer limited to reality as we know it but could reach higher levels of space, time, and consciousness, and actually "read" these records. This opened to him insights into virtually anything and everything imaginable.

In the language of the readings themselves, these sources are further described as follows:

(Q) From what source does this body Edgar Cayce derive its information?
(A) The information as given or obtained from this body is gathered from the sources from which the suggestion may derive its information. In this state the conscious mind becomes subjugated to the subconscious, super-conscious or soul mind; and may and does communicate with like minds, and the subconscious or soul force becomes universal. From any subconscious mind information may be obtained, either from this plane or from the impressions as left by the individuals that have gone on before . . .   3744-3

Upon time and space is written the thoughts, the deeds, the activities of an entity—as in relationships to its environs, its hereditary influence; as directed—or judgment drawn by or according to what the entity's ideal is. Hence, as it has been oft called, the record is God's book of remem-brance . . .   1650-1

More specific information about the Akashic records themselves is given in another reading:

. . . for, as records are made, the *akashic* records are as these: Activity of *any* nature, as of the voice, as of a light made, produced in the natural forces those of a motion—which pass on, or are upon, the record of that as time. As may be illustrated in the atomic vibration as set in motion for those in that called the audition, or the radio in its activity. *It* passes even faster than time itself. Hence *light* forces pass much faster, but the records are upon the *esoteric*, or etheric, or *akashic* forces, as they go along upon the wheels of time, the wings of time, or in *whatever* dimension we may signify as a matter of its momentum or movement. Hence as the forces that are attuned to those various incidents, periods, times, places, may be accorded to the record, the *contact* as of the needle upon the record, as to how clear a rendition or audition is received, or how clear or how perfect an *attunement* of the instrument used as the reproducer of same is attuned to those *keepers*—as may be termed—*of* those records.

What would be indicated by the keepers? That as just given, that they are the records upon the wings or the wheel of time itself. Time, as that as of space—as inter-between. That inter-between, that which is, that of which, that from one object to another when in matter is of the same nature, or what that is is what the other is, only changed in its vibration to produce that element, or that force, as is termed in man's terminology as *dimensions* of space, or *dimensions* that give it, whatever may be the solid, liquid, gas, or what *its form* or dimension!   364-6

Exploring the Readings

As to the content of the readings relating to the field of science, it's often been said that there are no true new discoveries as such. What is being "discovered" by scientists actually already exists in the cosmic scheme of things. In their search for knowledge and truth, they are simply led to find that which has always been there since the universe was brought into being. These too must be stored in the Akashic records and Cayce—having direct access to the records—was able to discuss topics about which he could not possibly have had any knowledge, given his limited education and the state of science at the time.

The author has performed an exhaustive scrutiny of the more than 14,000 Cayce readings looking for references relating to science in general and to those of the cosmos in particular—both for my own interest over the years and more recently in preparation for writing this book. Many of these findings are discussed elsewhere in the book. The readings were searched using more than a hundred different subjects and terms from astronomy, cosmology, and physics, as well as the names of specific celestial objects (planets, stars, etc.) and events (eclipses, conjunctions, etc.), and I was simply amazed at what turned up. Here was information given in readings that ranged from just a few "hits" per topic to well over a thousand in some cases!

However, there were also subjects much in the news today about which Cayce was strangely silent. These include such profound and exciting ones as the Big Bang, the expanding universe, neutron stars, pulsars, black holes, quasars, space–time warps, antimatter, and supernovae! But going back to what was said above, there's no question that these must be in the Akashic records as known universal concepts and that Edgar Cayce could have accessed them. The reason they don't appear in any of his readings seems obvious: *no one had asked him about them!* Just imagine if they had, many decades before astronomers even knew most of these things existed. I've often thought to myself, "If only Edgar were still alive today!" If he were, you would find me permanently camped out in Virginia Beach at the A.R.E.'s door.

An Astounding Revelation

Perhaps the most profound and incredible example (at least to me as an observational astronomer) of the hidden wonders contained within the Cayce material occurs in the following reading (the emphasis being mine):

> Before that we find the entity was in the land now called the Carpathian, during those periods when there was the exercising of activities in the land for the study of that which is professionally called in the present astrology or astronomy.
>
> For with the associations of the entity then with one Corpio, *an extended study was made through the abilities to use the glass that was found for the interpreting of the lights from the various heavenly bodies.*   1900-1

This certainly sounds as if someone back in those very ancient times had an optical telescope! And note especially the words "that was found"—what does that imply? According to science historians, the telescope as we know it today supposedly wasn't invented until the very early 1600s!

Yes, dear reader, the contents of Edgar Cayce's readings *are* utterly amazing! And yes, I've come to accept and embrace them as containing a treasure trove of advanced, esoteric scientific and technical knowledge for all truth seekers.

Index

Note that with few exceptions (including Cayce family members and their associates), people's names are listed only if they are actually quoted or referenced within the text itself. Also, many terms and proper names (especially in the case of the Sun, Moon, and various planets) are mentioned so frequently in the readings cited in this book that only their primary usage is given specific page numbers.

Edgar Cayce's A.R.E.

What is A.R.E.?

The Association for Research and Enlightenment, Inc., (A.R.E.©) was founded in 1931 to research and make available information on psychic development, dreams, holistic health, meditation, and life after death. As an open–membership research organization, the A.R.E. continues to study and publish such information, to initiate research, and to promote conferences, distance learning, and regional events. Edgar Cayce, the most documented psychic of our time, was the moving force in the establishment of A.R.E.

Who Was Edgar Cayce?

Edgar Cayce (1877–1945) was born on a farm near Hopkinsville, Ky. He was an average individual in most respects. Yet, throughout his life, he manifested one of the most remarkable psychic talents of all time. As a young man, he found that he was able to enter into a self–induced trance state, which enabled him to place his mind in contact with an unlimited source of information. While asleep, he could answer questions or give accurate discourses on any topic. These discourses, more than 14,000 in number, were transcribed as he spoke and are called "readings."

Given the name and location of an individual anywhere in the world, he could correctly describe a person's condition and outline a regiment of treatment. The consistent accuracy of his diagnoses and the effectiveness of the treatments he prescribed made him a medical phenomenon, and he came to be called the "father of holistic medicine."

Eventually, the scope of Cayce's readings expanded to include such subjects as world religions, philosophy, psychology, parapsychology, dreams, history, the missing years of Jesus, ancient civilizations, soul growth, psychic development, prophecy, and reincarnation.

A.R.E. Membership

People from all walks of life have discovered meaningful and life–transforming insights through membership in A.R.E. To learn more about Edgar Cayce's A.R.E. and how membership in the A.R.E. can enhance your life, visit our web site at EdgarCayce.org, or call us toll–free at 800–333–4499.

Edgar Cayce's A.R.E.
215 67th Street
Virginia Beach, VA 23451–2061

EDGARCAYCE.ORG

ABOUT THE AUTHOR

The author shown with his 5–inch Celestron Schmidt–Cassegrain catadioptric telescope. This compact state–of–the–art instrument is capable of showing the A.R.E. complex if it were placed on the Moon a quarter of a million miles away! Thousands of people of all ages have viewed the wonders of the heavens through it—many of them while attending A.R.E. conferences.

James Mullaney is an astronomy writer, lecturer, and consultant who has published more than five hundred articles and five books on observing the wonders of the heavens, and logged over twenty thousand hours of stargazing time with the unaided eye, binoculars, and telescopes. Formerly Curator of the Buhl Planetarium and Institute of Popular Science in Pittsburgh and more recently Director of the DuPont Planetarium, he served as staff astronomer at the University of Pittsburgh's Allegheny Observatory and as an editor for *Sky & Telescope*, *Astronomy*, and *Star & Sky* magazines. Mullaney was one of the contributors to Carl Sagan's award–winning *Cosmos* PBS television series; his work has received recognition from such notables (and fellow stargazers) as Sir Arthur Clarke, Johnny Carson, Ray Bradbury, Dr. Wernher von Braun, and former student—NASA scientist/astronaut Dr. Jay Apt. His fifty–year mission as a "celestial evangelist" has been to *Celebrate the Universe!*—to get others to look up at the majesty of the night sky and personally experience the joys of stargazing. In February 2005 he was elected a Fellow of the prestigious Royal Astronomical Society of London.